A Culinary Collection

A COOKBOOK FROM

THE DETROIT INSTITUTE OF ARTS

The Detroit Institute of Arts

5200 Woodward Avenue, Detroit, Michigan 48202

Editor: Judith A. Ruskin
Editorial Assistant: Kelli Carr
Director of Photography: Dirk Bakker

Produced by Meadows Design Office Inc., Washington, D.C.
T/A Meadows Press, www.mdomedia.com
Designer: Marc Alain Meadows
Illustration Editor: Amy Frenkil Meadows
Copywriter: Lee Fleming

Library of Congress Cataloging in Publication Data is available.
ISBN 0-89558-154-X

Cover: *Michigan Fruits and Vegetables,* detail, east wall, *Detroit Industry,* 1932,
Diego Rivera, Mexican; fresco, 26¾ x 72⅞ in. (68 x 185 cm). Gift of Edsel B. Ford
(33.10).

Endleaves: *Fowl and Melons,* detail, ca. 1970, Sisson Blanchard, Haitian; oil on
canvas, 43½ x 62 in. (110.5 x 157.5 cm). Founders Society Purchase, Modern
Paintings Fund (1990.272). Reproduced with permission of Roland Wiener and
family.

Page one: *Tureen with Lid, Liner, and Stand,* 1733/34, Thomas Germain, French;
silver, 10 x 21½ x 16¼ in. (25.4 x 54.6 x 41.3 cm). Founders Society Purchase,
Elizabeth Parke Firestone Collection of Early French Silver Fund (59.18).

Frontispiece: *Dinner Silverware Set,* ca. 1906, Josef Hoffmann, Austrian;
silverplate, 8⅜ in. (21.3 cm). Founders Society Purchase, Benson and Edith Ford
Fund and Mr. and Mrs. Alvan Macauley, Jr., Fund (1985.33).

Contents: *Hommage à Claudel,* detail, ca. 1970, Georges Auguste, Haitian; oil on
canvas, 40 x 50 in. (101.6 x 127 cm). Gift of Aubelin Jolicoeur Claire Gallery.
(F1984.61) Reproduced with permission of Roland Wiener and family.

Colophon, page 160: *Menu,* ca. 1908, Ethel Mars, American; woodcut, 7⅞ x 9¾ in.
(20 x 24.8 cm). Founders Society Purchase, Elizabeth P. Kirby Fund, Hal H. Smith
Fund, John S. Newberry Fund, Charles L. Freer Fund (1997.71)

Printed in China

To Margie Gillis

for her lifelong support and dedication to

the Detroit Institute of Arts

Contents

Director's Foreword

It has been fifteen years since the publication of the first Detroit Institute of Arts cookbook—*A Visual Feast*. Sam Sachs became director of the museum just before the publication of that book, and I took on the post in September 1999, in time for this cookbook. Although I only recently started my tenure as director of the Detroit Institute of Arts, I am struck by how much has changed during that time, both at the museum and in the community. At the DIA, a new governance and management structure was put in place, bringing us more into line with our peer institutions, and a major capital campaign has been launched to completely renovate both the original 1920s building and the north and south wings, added some thirty-five years ago. Many gifts, epitomized by a van Gogh portrait and a Degas landscape, greatly enhanced the continually growing permanent collection. The 1997 exhibition "Splendors of Ancient Egypt" set all-time attendance records, only to be itself surpassed by "Van Gogh: Face to Face" in the spring of 2000.

Significant changes also occurred in the city of Detroit during the last fifteen years. Dennis Archer succeeded long-time Detroit mayor Coleman Young as the city's leader; General Motors moved their headquarters from the city's New Center to downtown's Renaissance Center; and the old Hudson's Building came down. The Fox Theater on Woodward Avenue reopened after painstaking renovation to anchor the city's burgeoning theater district; the Detroit Opera Theater moved into a grand performance space of its own; and the Detroit Symphony Orchestra returned to its historic home in Orchestra Hall.

With all of the changes, both in the museum and outside its walls, a crucial constant—art—remains. Even here, though, there is much gratifying change. Just as the recipes included here are new, the art works selected to accompany them are different from those of the earlier cookbook. Many of the objects, in fact, were acquired by the DIA in the interval between books. The recipes, gathered from the museum's many friends, volunteers, and staff reflect different cultures and run the gamut of cooking occasions: comfort foods, meals for informal gatherings and celebrations, elegant fare for more for-

Café Scene in Paris, detail, 1877, Henri Gervex, French; oil on canvas, 39⅜ x 55½ in. (100.5 x 156 cm). Founders Society Purchase, Robert H. Tannahill Foundation Fund (1992.8). © 2000 Artists Rights Society (ARS), New York/ADAGP, Paris.

mal events, and desserts both plain and fancy. Similarly, the art, made in places as disparate as Africa and Alaska, ranges from paintings to sculpture; prints to ceramics; and ancient works to the most contemporary.

This book would not have been possible without the tireless work of the Cookbook Committee, ably chaired by Jane Solomon and Margie Gillis. The committee took on the responsibility of collecting the recipes and testing them all for accuracy and, of course, taste. The proceeds of the sale of this cookbook will be used to further the development and publication of books and other materials intended for children and their families.

It is most appropriate that this book be dedicated to Margie Gillis for her unstinting work on both cookbooks and for her many years of devoted service to the Detroit Institute of Arts. Margie has brought a sense of graciousness to all of her museum undertakings, from the elegant receptions and banquets she organized with the Women's Committee to the lovely flower arrangements she created for the "Art and Flowers: A Festival of Spring" displays. Margie joined the Founders Society Board of Trustees in 1958 and served in a variety of capacities, including secretary and vice president, for the next twenty-eight years. In 1986, she became a lifetime trustee and is now a director emeritus of the recently reconfigured Board of Directors. We thank her for her generosity and many years of service and look forward to continuing to work with her in the years ahead.

I hope that the recipes in this book will inspire you to great artistry in the kitchen, and that the many masterpieces illustrated here will remind you to come often to the Detroit Institute of Arts to explore one of this country's great collections.

Graham W. J. Beal
Director

Acknowledgments

The effort to produce a second museum cookbook was spearheaded by the Cookbook Committee. Without the commitment and dedication of these volunteers, *A Culinary Collection* would never have become a reality. Committee members solicited recipes, divided them into appropriate groups, and tested each one before including the final version in the book. Special thanks go to the committee chairs who, along with the two chairs of the testing committee, kept the project on track, gathering and organizing the recipes and taste testings. Our appreciation also goes to following hardworking committee members:

Margie Gillis and Jane Solomon, Chairs
Carolyn Schreiber and Joyce Siegel, Testing Committee Assistant Chairs

Martha Beechler
Tula Georgeson
Rosalind Grand
Joyce Harding

Lucie Kelly
Liz Kuhlman
Ruth Lefkowitz
Sandra Moers

Raquel Ross
Ruth Waldfogel

Marc Meadows, of Meadows Design Office, designed this cookbook, as he had the previous one. At the Detroit Institute of Arts, the book was edited by Judith Ruskin with the assistance of Kelli Carr. Maria Santangelo of the Department of European Sculpture and Decorative Arts, a cooking whiz in her own right, provided expert advice on recipes, measurements, ingredients, and other culinary matters. Last, but perhaps most important, are all the museum's supporters and staff who generously shared their recipes with us, for without their contributions, there would have been no second Detroit Institute of Arts cookbook.

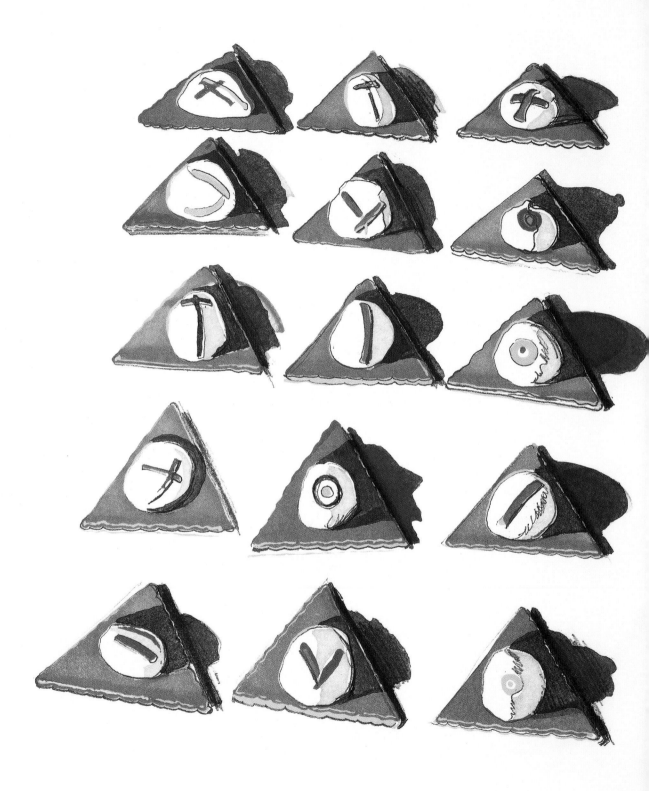

Appetizers and First Courses

Whether orchestrated on a repoussé silver platter in the classic French style, or striking a more rustic note in primitive clay bowls and earthenware, appetizers are a wake-up call to the palate, stimulating our taste buds and enlivening any gathering. Around the world, in almost every culture, some kind of canapé is served before the main meal—although just when and where the custom began is still unclear. One thing is certain: Whether appearing as elegantly wrapped asparagus spears, zesty bean-filled quesadillas, grilled vegetables, or delicate rolls of smoked fish, these tidbits are pledged to one purpose—priming our senses for the gustatory delights that will follow..

~

Triangle Thins, 1971, Wayne Thiebaud, American; softground etching and aquatint printed in color on wove paper, 29¾ x 22 in. (75.5 x 55.8 cm). Gift of J. L. Hudson Gallery (74.154). © Wayne Thiebaud/Licensed by VAGA, New York.

Apristachios

dried apricot halves, pitted

chèvre cheese

pistachios, roasted, unsalted,
  and shelled

Spread a small amount of cheese on the inside of the apricot halves. Top with pistachios. Can also be served as a dessert. It's fun to let your guests make their own.

John Beechler

Asparagus in Flour Tortillas

1 teaspoon olive oil

2–3 bunches asparagus,
  cut into spears, about 3–4
  inches long

2–3 red sweet peppers, cut in
  strips same length as
  asparagus

2–3 Portobello mushroom
  caps, cut in slices similar in
  shape to peppers

½ vegetable or chicken
  bouillon cube

2–3 tablespoons water

1 package of 10 tortillas

sweet hot mustard

In large frying pan, sauté asparagus spears, red pepper strips, and mushrooms in olive oil 2–3 minutes. Add water and bring to a boil; crumble in one-half of vegetable or chicken bouillon. Stir 3–4 minutes until dissolved. Vegetables should be slightly soft, but still firm and colorful. Liquid should be reduced to almost nothing. Spread tortillas with mustard. Cut tortillas into 6 pie-shaped pieces. Roll one asparagus spear, one red pepper strip, and one mushroom strip inside one tortilla. Serve at room temperature or heated in microwave 1–2 minutes.

NUMBER OF SPEARS DETERMINES NUMBER OF APPETIZERS

Susan Miller

Still Life, 1644, Pieter Claesz, Dutch; paint on wood panel, 17¼ x 21 in. (43.8 x 53.3 cm).

Founders Society Purchase, General Membership Fund (40.129).

Bacon Tomato Cups

1 10-ounce can buttermilk
  biscuits

⅓ cup cooked, crumbled
  bacon

1 14-ounce can diced
  tomatoes, drained well

1 small onion, chopped

3 ounces Swiss cheese, finely
  grated

½ cup mayonnaise

1 teaspoon dried basil

Preheat oven to 375° F.

Divide each raw biscuit into thirds; press into mini-muffin tins. Combine all other ingredients and fill cups equally.

Bake 15 minutes.

MAKES 30 PIECES

Kathleen McCarroll, M.D.

Smoked Fish Appetizer Roll

1 pound smoked whitefish,
  boned and flaked

1 8-ounce package cream
  cheese, room temperature

1 tablespoon lemon juice

2 teaspoons onion, grated

1 teaspoon horseradish

2 tablespoons parsley, chopped

1 teaspoon liquid smoke
  (optional)

salt to taste

½ cup pecans, chopped

In a large bowl, combine fish, cream cheese, lemon juice, grated onion, horseradish, parsley, liquid smoke, and salt. Mix thoroughly by hand. Chill a few hours. Shape into a log and roll in nuts.

Serve with rounds of breads or crackers.

SERVES 6–10

Mildred Young

Black Bean Quesadillas

1 15-ounce can black beans,
   rinsed and drained
1 teaspoon cumin
1 teaspoon cayenne
1 teaspoon chili powder
1 small red onion, quartered
1 cup cilantro, packed
2 jalapeño peppers, fresh
4 medium flour tortillas
1 cup Monterey Jack cheese,
   shredded
1–2 avocados, sliced, sprinkled
   with lemon juice
vegetable oil for cooking

SALSA

1 small tomato, chopped
2 tablespoons cilantro,
   chopped

¼ cup Spanish onion, chopped
lime juice to taste
fresh jalapeño peppers,
   minced, to taste

Reserve ¼ cup black beans. Place remainder of black beans with cumin, cayenne, chili powder, onion, cilantro, and jalapeño peppers in food processor; chop finely. Place mixture in a small bowl. Add reserved whole black beans and mix well.

Prepare salsa, mixing together in a small bowl the tomato, cilantro, Spanish onion, lime juice, and jalapeño peppers.

On half of each flour tortilla, layer one quarter of black bean mixture, cheese, salsa, and avocado slices. Fold tortilla and transfer to pan with heated oil. Cook both sides at medium heat until cheese has melted and tortillas are golden.

SERVES 4

Nancy Barr

Large Plate, 1988, Jane Bruce, American; blown glass with pastel and sandblasted etching, 30 in. (76.2 cm).

Gift of the Jack A. and Aviva Robinson Collection (1996.137).

Herring Antipasto

1 16-ounce jar herring in wine, drained, cut in strips
1 green pepper, diced
1 red pepper, diced
1 medium red onion, chopped
1 6-ounce can black olives, sliced
1 12-ounce bottle chili sauce
1 6-ounce jar marinated artichoke hearts, drained and chopped

Mix all ingredients together and refrigerate 24 hours. Serve with pumpernickel bread. Will keep in refrigerator for weeks.

Mildred Young

Mozzarella and Tomato Antipasto

3 tablespoons olive oil, divided
12 thin slices of baguette (French bread)
3 ripe plum tomatoes, thinly sliced crosswise
dried oregano
salt and fresh ground pepper to taste
10 ounces mozzarella cheese
12 anchovy fillets in olive oil, drained (optional)

Preheat oven to 350° F.

Using 2 tablespoons of olive oil brush one side of each baguette slice. Lay bread slices, oiled side up, on a baking sheet. Place tomato slices in a shallow dish and sprinkle with one tablespoon olive oil, oregano, salt, and pepper and toss gently. Cut mozzarella into 12 thin slices and place on bread. If desired, place anchovy fillet on top of cheese. Arrange one or two tomato slices on top. Place in oven and bake until bread is thoroughly heated and mozzarella is almost melted, about 5 minutes.

SERVES 6

Dianne Cornell

Broiled Portobello Mushrooms

8 Portobello mushrooms

½ cup balsamic vinegar

3 tablespoons fresh cilantro, chopped (optional)

2 garlic cloves, coarsely chopped

1 teaspoon salt

½ teaspoon pepper

1 cup olive oil

Clean mushrooms with soft brush or damp cloth. Remove stems and discard.

Prepare marinade by mixing together the vinegar, cilantro, garlic, salt, and pepper. Gradually whisk in the olive oil until mixture is thickened. Brush mushrooms all over with marinade, reserving extra marinade to use as a basting sauce.

Arrange mushrooms, gill side up, in a shallow dish. Cover loosely and refrigerate 4–6 hours.

Preheat broiler. Place mushrooms on an upper rack and broil 3–4 minutes per side, or until tender, basting frequently with reserved marinade.

Arrange on a large platter or individual serving dishes.

MAKES 8 PIECES

Ruth Waldfogel

Still Life with Carafe, Knife, and Chestnuts, 1918, Diego Rivera, Mexican; pencil on paper, 12⅛ x 9⁵⁄₁₆ in. (31.4 x 23.3 cm). Bequest of Robert H. Tannahill (70.333).

Rivera-18-

Marinated Red Sweet Peppers

2 large sweet red peppers

2 tablespoons pesto without
   cheese

fresh garlic, minced, to taste

salt and pepper to taste

½ cup Italian dressing

4 small Italian plum or yellow
   tomatoes, peeled, seeded,
   and diced into small pieces

8 Kalamata or other black
   olives such as niçoise, pitted
   and cut into slivers

Broil peppers until skins blister; plunge into cold water and peel. Cut open, remove seeds and membrane, and cut into narrow strips.

Place peppers in a shallow dish and cover with pesto. Sprinkle with seasonings and add three-quarters of the dressing a little at a time until peppers are well moistened but not floating. Cover and refrigerate, turning once or twice, for at least 12 hours.

Combine the tomatoes and olives with remaining dressing, tossing well; cover and refrigerate. One hour before serving, drain the marinade from both tomato-olive mixture and peppers. Combine and gently toss.

SERVES 4

Ruth Waldfogel

Patera, 5th/4th century B.C., Etruscan; bronze, diameter with handle 15¼ in. (38.7 cm). Gift of Mrs. Lillian Henkel Haass (51.72).

Scallops and Avocado with Red Pepper Sauce

1 ½ pounds sea scallops rinsed, sinew removed, and sliced into 3 slices each

½ cup lemon juice

salt and pepper to taste

1 ½ pounds red pepper, charred, peeled, and cooled

2 tablespoons olive oil

¼ teaspoon cayenne

1 teaspoon salt

2 large avocados, well ripened, sliced

Marinate scallops in lemon juice and salt and pepper for 6–8 hours.

Place peppers in food processor. Slowly add olive oil, cayenne, and salt. Divide pepper sauce onto six chilled plates. Slice avocados in thirds, leaving narrow end intact. Fan out the avocado; place on sauce. Remove slices of scallops from marinade and blot on paper towel to remove excess marinade. Place scallops over narrow end of avocado.

SERVES 6

Corliss Rosenberg

Shrimp De Jonghe

½ pound butter

½ cup lemon juice

2 cloves garlic, minced

2 tablespoons chives, chopped

2 tablespoons parsley, chopped

2 teaspoons Worcestershire sauce

1 pound jumbo shrimp, boiled and deveined

1 cup seasoned bread crumbs

6 tablespoons dry Sauterne

In skillet, melt butter; add lemon juice, garlic, chives, parsley, and Worcestershire sauce. Add shrimp and stir 2–3 minutes. Add bread crumbs and stir well. Blend in Sauterne, stirring approximately 1 minute.

Serve in individual shells or in a chafing dish.

SERVES 4

Melvy Erman Lewis

SOUPS, STEWS, AND CHILIES

oup is. . . the comestible that stands alone, a meal in it-self. Soup is. . . . the complement (or contrast) to the main event, herald of the approaching entrée. Both visions of this most versatile food apply–and no wonder: Soup's role as a culinary staple predates our written history. Over millennia, cultures around the world have invented and refined not only memorable recipes but also innovative ways to present these satisfying concoctions. The elaborate patterns of Ming porcelain bowls and saucers, the simplicity of spoons and porringers fashioned by Native Americans– all pay tribute to form and function, the serving up of wonderful soups. Whether delicate and cooling for summer dinners alfresco, or hot and hearty for winter repasts by the fire, the soups, stews and chilies in these pages are truly "comfort" foods and artful palate-pleasers.

≈

In the Fields, detail, ca. 1878–80, Eastman Johnson, American; oil on board, 17¾ x 27½ in. (45.1 x 69.9 cm).

Founders Society Purchase, Dexter M. Ferry Fund (58.1).

Spring Asparagus Soup

2 tablespoons butter

2 medium onions, chopped

3 garlic cloves, chopped

2 pounds asparagus, cut into
   1-inch pieces, reserving tips

4 carrots, peeled and chopped

1 cup parsley, chopped, stems
   removed

¼ teaspoon dried thyme

3 bay leaves

½ cup fresh basil, chopped

6 cups chicken stock

salt and pepper

2 plum tomatoes, seeded and
   chopped

Melt the butter in a stockpot and cook the onions and garlic over medium heat until soft. Add the asparagus, carrots, parsley, thyme, bay leaves, basil, and chicken stock. Bring to boil and reduce heat to simmer. Cook over low heat for 35 minutes. Cool. Remove bay leaves and purée the vegetables in a processor; return to pot. Reheat over medium heat and add salt and pepper to taste. Add the reserved asparagus tips and cook for 5 minutes. Ladle into bowls and top with chopped tomato.

SERVES 8

Maureen D'Avanzo

Cup Stand, 1568/1644, Chinese, Ming Dynasty; laquer with mother-of-pearl inlay, 3⅛ x 3½ in. (7.8 x 8.8 cm). Founders Society Purchase, G. Albert Lyon Foundation Fund and L. A. Young Fund (80.26).

Sopa Azteca

6 tortillas cut into thin strips

1 whole chicken breast

2 quarts chicken broth

1 tablespoon oil

1 medium onion, diced

1 clove garlic, crushed

2 medium tomatoes, peeled
and chopped

1 pimento or red sweet bell
pepper, julienned

2–4 chilies (jalapeño or
Serrano), diced

1–2 sliced avocados, diced

2 tablespoons farmers cheese

2 tablespoons cilantro or
parsley, chopped

Preheat oven to 350° F.

Bake the tortilla strips in oven 10–15 minutes until crisp but not brown.

Poach the chicken breast in the chicken broth; cool, remove, and shred, reserving the chicken broth. Sauté the onion and garlic in oil until soft; add the tomatoes, pimento, and chilies and cook until the mixture becomes a sauce. Return the chicken to the broth. Add tomato mixture and cook 10–15 minutes.

Remove from heat and garnish with avocado, cheese, cilantro or parsley, and tortilla strips.

SERVES 8

Joy Emery

Cold Cucumber Soup

3 cucumbers, peeled and seeded

2 bunches scallions, cleaned

1 pint sour cream or yogurt

salt, white pepper, and garlic
powder to taste

1 quart buttermilk

2 tablespoons lemon juice

parsley, chopped

Combine cucumber and scallions in a processor or blender and purée until smooth. Transfer to a large bowl and whisk in sour cream or yogurt and seasonings. Add buttermilk and lemon juice; mix and chill overnight to develop flavors. Garnish with chopped parsley.

SERVES 8

Curl Tutag

Black Bean Soup with Pico de Gallo

1 pound black beans, soaked
   in water for 30 minutes
5 cups chicken broth
¼ cup ham, chopped
1 onion, chopped
1 garlic clove, minced
1 tablespoon oil
salt and pepper to taste
sour cream
cilantro or parsley, chopped
tortilla chips

Drain beans; cover again with water and cook 1–2 hours until tender. Drain and purée in processor or blender, adding chicken broth. Set aside. In large pan, sauté ham, onion, and garlic in oil. Remove excess drippings and add beans and chicken broth. Reheat, season to taste, and serve with a dollop of sour cream, chopped parsley or cilantro, tortilla chips, and pico de gallo relish.

PICO DE GALLO RELISH

¼ cup red onion, finely chopped
2 oranges, peeled, thinly sliced crosswise, saving juice
½ cucumber cut in half lengthwise, thinly sliced
½ jicama, peeled and cut into matchsticks
½ bell pepper, seeded and cut into matchsticks
2 tablespoons olive oil
1 tablespoon white wine vinegar
⅛ teaspoon each: salt, cayenne pepper, and oregano
½ teaspoon red pepper flakes
¼ cup orange juice

For relish, mix together onion, oranges, cucumber, jicama, and bell pepper in a large bowl. Combine remaining relish ingredients in a small bowl and pour over vegetable and fruit mixture. Adjust seasonings to taste.

SERVES 8

Pat Wasson

Carrot Ginger Soup

2 tablespoons oil or butter

1 medium onion, chopped

1½ pounds carrots, peeled and
   sliced (about 12)

2 cups water

8 ounces cream cheese

½ cup frozen orange juice concentrate

3-inch generous piece fresh
   ginger, peeled and sliced
   thinly across the grain

3–4 cups chicken stock

¼ cup dry sherry (optional)

In a 4-quart pan, sauté onions in oil or butter until translucent. Add carrots and water. Simmer until tender, 15–20 minutes. Add cheese, orange concentrate, and ginger. Stir to melt cheese. In processor or blender, purée one-third of the mixture at a time. (Soup concentrate base may be frozen at this point for future use.)

When ready to serve, add chicken stock and sherry and heat. May also be served ice cold in a goblet.

SERVES 6–8

Phyllis McLean

Gazpacho

4 tomatoes, chopped

1 green pepper, chopped

2 stalks celery, chopped

1 small cucumber, chopped

1 small onion, chopped

2 cloves garlic, minced

¼ cup parsley

3 tablespoons wine vinegar

2 tablespoons olive oil

1 teaspoon salt

¼ teaspoon pepper

1 teaspoon Worcestershire
   sauce

46 ounces canned tomato juice

Combine the vegetables, garlic, and parsley in a large container. Add all remaining ingredients and stir until thoroughly combined. Chill at least 4 hours.

Serve with bread sticks.

SERVES 12   *Alma Rand*

Cream of Fennel Soup

¼ cup extra virgin olive oil

4 fennel bulbs cut into ¼-inch
   strips, discard outer stalk
   and reserve ½ cup finely
   chopped greens

6 cups chicken broth

1 cup heavy whipping cream

GARLIC CROUTONS

1½ tablespoons butter

1½ tablespoons extra virgin
   olive oil

1 clove garlic, sliced

½ cup French bread cubes

Heat olive oil in a large pot. Put fennel in the hot oil and cover with broth, bringing to a boil. Reduce heat to simmer. Cook partially covered until fennel is well cooked and falls apart, about 50 minutes. Cool and purée in a processor or blender. Strain through a sieve to remove strings. Return puréed soup to the pot; add heavy cream and the reserved chopped greens. Reheat, stirring occasionally (do not cover). Serve with garlic croutons on top.

Heat oil and butter and sauté garlic until golden. Remove garlic, add bread cubes, and sauté until golden. Serve on top of soup.

SERVES 4–6   *Roselyn Litman*

The Cook (La cuisinière), 1775, Giovanni David, Italian; etching and aquatint, 9½ x 6½ in. (24.1 x 16.6 cm). Founders Society Purchase, Benson and Edith Ford Fund (73.172.10).

Minestrone Soup

4 tablespoons butter

¾ cup onion, chopped

¼ cup celery, chopped

⅓ cup carrots, chopped

1 19-ounce can white kidney
  beans (cannellini), rinsed
  and drained

1 cup zucchini, sliced

½ cup cabbage, shredded

½ cup canned Italian
  tomatoes with liquid

1½ cup baking potatoes, cubed
  (about 2 potatoes)

1 quart chicken broth

2 cloves garlic, chopped

2 teaspoons parsley, chopped

½ teaspoon dried basil

½ teaspoon salt

¼ teaspoon cracked black
  pepper

⅓ cup elbow macaroni

½ cup Parmesan cheese,
  grated

Melt butter in a deep, heavy soup pot. Sauté onion, celery, and carrots for 5 minutes. Add beans, vegetables, stock, and spices. Bring to a boil, then reduce heat and simmer 1 hour. Add macaroni. Stirring slowly, add ¼ cup cheese and simmer an additional 30 minutes. Adjust seasoning and garnish with remaining cheese.

SERVES 6–8

Jane Solomon

Spoon, ca. 1890, Chippewa, Wisconsin; wood (maple), 3½ x 12⅛ x 9¾ in. (8.9 x 30.8 x 24.8 cm). Founders Society Purchase (81.665).

Hungarian Paprika Soup

1 pound ground beef

2 cups onion, chopped

1½ quarts beef stock

1½ tablespoons paprika

1 8-ounce can tomato sauce

2 cups celery, chopped

2 cups carrots, chopped

1 tablespoon butter

1 tablespoon flour

1 cup egg noodles

salt, pepper, and cayenne to
   taste

sour cream to garnish

Brown meat and onions in a large heavy pot. Add stock, paprika, and tomato sauce. Simmer 30 minutes, covered. Add celery and carrots and cook until tender, 20–30 minutes. In separate pan, melt butter, mix with flour and cook briefly. Add enough flour to thicken the soup to desired consistency. Add noodles. Simmer until noodles are cooked. Add more liquid if too thick and adjust seasoning to taste. Serve with a dollop of sour cream.

SERVES 6–8

Margie Gillis

Potato Leek Soup

3 tablespoons butter

1 cup sliced leeks, white part
   only

½ cup onions, chopped

2–3 potatoes, peeled and diced
   (1½ pounds)

6 cups chicken stock

salt and pepper to taste

chopped parsley

Melt the butter in a large saucepan over medium heat. Add leeks and onions and cook 5 minutes until tender. Add potatoes, chicken stock, salt, and pepper. Cover and simmer over low heat, about 20 minutes. Pour soup into a processor and blend until smooth. Return to pan and reheat. Ladle into bowls and sprinkle with parsley.

SERVES 4–6

Caroline Ashleigh

Red Pepper Soup with Pear

4 tablespoons olive oil

8 red peppers, seeded and
  sliced thin

3 carrots, peeled and sliced
  thin

3 shallots, peeled and sliced
  thin

1 clove garlic, peeled and
  sliced thin

1 pear, peeled, quartered, and
  sliced thin

1 quart chicken stock

1 teaspoon crushed, dried red
  pepper

dash of cayenne pepper
  (optional)

salt and pepper to taste

sprigs of fresh tarragon for
  garnish

½ cup sour cream or yogurt

Heat the oil in a large skillet and sauté the sliced vegetables, garlic, and pear over medium heat until tender, 8–10 minutes. Add the stock, dried red pepper, cayenne pepper, salt, and pepper. Bring to a slow boil and simmer 25–30 minutes, covered. Purée in a processor and pour back in pan to reheat. Garnish with fresh tarragon and a dollop of sour cream or yogurt.

SERVES 4–6

Andrew Camden

Cottage with Milkmaid, ca. 1780, Anonymous, English; earthenware with polychrome decoration, 7 x 8 x 5½ in. (17.8 x 20.3 x 14 cm). Founders Society Purchase, Benson and Edith Ford Fund (76.69).

Pumpkin Soup

6 small pumpkins, 8 inches
  round

1 pound sweet yams, peeled
  and diced

1 pound carrots, peeled and
  diced

1 tablespoon oil

1 small onion

1½ quarts chicken stock

3 garlic cloves, pressed

¾ teaspoon cinnamon

¾ teaspoon allspice

1 teaspoon salt

pepper to taste

2 cups sour cream

chopped parsley

Preheat oven to 350 F.

Remove tops from pumpkins, cutting into the pulp. Parboil the pumpkins until the pulp is soft. Scoop out pulp, leaving a ¾-inch wall. Separate the seeds from the pulp; toast seeds in oven on a baking sheet 15–20 minutes and set aside.

Process the pulp with the yams and carrots until lumpy and place in a large soup kettle. Heat oil in a skillet, sauté onions until softened and add to pumpkin mixture. Add stock to cover pulp mixture. Add garlic, cloves, cinnamon, and allspice and cook uncovered over medium heat until reduced by half. Simmer until ready to serve.

Just before serving, fold in 1½ cups sour cream. Ladle mixture into pumpkin shells; put a dollop of sour cream on each and sprinkle generously with pumpkin seeds and chopped parsley. Cover with pumpkin tops if desired.

SERVES 6

A. Alfred Taubman

Baked Butternut Squash Soup

2 pounds butternut squash, peeled, seeded, and cut into 1-inch rounds

2 large carrots, peeled and cut into 1-inch rounds

1 medium onion, cut into chunks

3 cups chicken or vegetable broth

¼ teaspoon each mace, ground ginger, cinnamon, and allspice

¼ teaspoon salt

¼ teaspoon fresh ground pepper

2 teaspoons honey

sour cream or yogurt (optional)

Preheat oven to 400° F.

Place all vegetables, broth, and seasonings in a covered, ovenproof dish. Drizzle with honey and bake 45–50 minutes, until vegetables are tender. Remove and pureé in a blender or food processor. If desired, garnish with a dollop of sour cream or yogurt.

SERVES 4–6

Janet Miller

∽

The Kitchen of a Montparnasse Bistro, Paris, 1929, André Kertész, American; gelatin silver print, 9⅞ x 8 in. (25.2 x 20.5 cm). Gift of Mr. and Mrs. Noel Levine (F1985.168).

Vegetable Lentil Soup

1 cup red lentils

2 potatoes, cubed

4–6 carrots, peeled

2–3 parsnips, peeled

2 stalks celery

2 onions

3 Knorr vegetarian bouillon
   cubes

6 cups water

½ ounce dry mushrooms

Place all ingredients in a 6-quart pot. Bring to a boil. Lower heat and simmer 1½–2 hours. Remove from broth and purée carrots, parsnips, celery, and onions in food processor or blender with some of the soup broth. Leave the cubed potatoes in the soup. Return vegetable purée to the rest of the soup. Serve hot.

SERVES 6–8

Rosalind Grand

Wild Rice Soup

1 tablespoon onion, minced

6 tablespoons butter

½ cup flour

3 cups chicken broth

2 cups cooked wild rice

⅓ cup ham or turkey, minced

½ cup carrot, finely grated

3 tablespoons almonds, sliced
   and chopped

½ teaspoon salt

1 cup half-and-half

2 tablespoons sherry

Sauté onion in butter until soft. Blend in flour and cook for 1 minute. Slowly stir in chicken broth and boil 1 minute. Add rice, meat, carrot, almonds, and salt and simmer 5 minutes. Add half-and-half and sherry. Bring back to a simmer and serve.

SERVES 6

Helen McKnight

Bowl, ca. 1850, Chippewa, Michigan; carved ash, 19 x 13⅛ x 8¼ in. (48.3 x 33.3 x 21 cm). Founders Society Purchase with funds from Flint Ink Corporation (81.748).

Super Bowl Stew

3 whole skinless, boneless
   chicken breasts, split
1 cup chicken broth
splash of sherry (optional)
1 cup onion, chopped
1 green pepper, chopped
2 cloves garlic, minced
2 14½-ounce cans stewed
   tomatoes
¾ cup medium to hot picante
   sauce
1 teaspoon chili powder
1 teaspoon cumin
½ teaspoon salt
1 15-ounce can of pinto beans,
   drained

Cut chicken into 1-inch strips and cook in chicken broth and sherry until chicken loses its pink color. Remove chicken from broth and set aside. In broth, cook onion, green pepper, garlic, stewed tomatoes, picante sauce, and spices for 10 minutes. Stir in beans and cook another 5 minutes. Add chicken to mixture and cook 5 more minutes.

To serve, ladle into bowls. May also be served over rice or with toppings.

SUGGESTED ACCOMPANIMENTS

Rice, shredded cheddar cheese, sliced avocados, sour cream, cut green scallions.

SERVES 8–10

Cele Landay

Chili

3 garlic cloves, minced

2 tablespoons vegetable oil

4 pounds ground veal or
  ground chicken

6 large onions, sliced

4 large green peppers, chopped
  coarsely

3 16-ounce cans tomatoes

4 16-ounce cans red kidney
  beans, drained

¼ cup chili powder

1 teaspoon white vinegar

3 dashes cayenne pepper

3 whole cloves

1 bay leaf

salt and pepper to taste

In a large frying pan, cook garlic in oil until golden. Add veal or chicken and cook for 10 minutes, breaking up with a fork so it browns evenly. Remove meat from frying pan and set aside. Remove excess drippings from pan; add onions and peppers and sauté until tender. In a large soup pot, add all ingredients and stir well. Cover and cook over low heat for 1 hour; If too thick, add additional tomatoes; if too thin, uncover and simmer longer.

SERVES 12

Margot Coville

The Lunch Counter, **1927, Martin Lewis, American; drypoint printed in brown ink, 6⅞ x 9⅞ in. (17.4 x 25.1 cm). Gift of Mr. Robert M. Katzman and Mrs. Lisa Katzman in honor of Sidney and Betty Katzman and their children, Ellen and Laura, from the collection assembled by Patricia Lewis (T1991.145).**

Three Bean Chili

3 cloves garlic, minced

1 tablespoon olive or cooking oil

1 28-ounce can Italian style tomatoes, cut up

2 cups water

1 12-ounce can tomato paste

1 tablespoon Dijon-style mustard

1 tablespoon chili powder

1 teaspoon crushed, dried basil

1 teaspoon crushed, dried oregano

1–1½ teaspoons ground cumin

½ teaspoon black pepper

1 15-ounce can red kidney beans, drained

1 15-ounce can Great Northern beans, drained

1 15-ounce can chickpeas (garbanzo beans), drained

1 cup carrot, chopped

1 cup corn kernels, fresh or frozen

1 cup zucchini, chopped

several dashes of bottled hot pepper sauce (optional)

¾ cup Parmesan or cheddar cheese, shredded

In Dutch oven or large enameled pot, cook garlic in hot oil for 30 seconds. Stir in undrained tomatoes, water, tomato paste, mustard, and spices. Add beans and bring mixture to boil. Reduce heat; simmer covered for 10 minutes or more. Stir in vegetables and simmer covered 20 minutes or more, until vegetables are tender. Add pepper sauce to taste.

Ladle into serving bowls and top each serving with two tablespoons grated cheese.

SERVES 6

Helen Gay

SALADS, DRESSINGS, AND CONDIMENTS

*T*hink beyond basics when it comes to contemporary salads. Their many forms embrace a wealth of ingredients, depending on the season and the garden's bounty: crisp greens and vibrant vegetables, molded blends of fruit and nuts, seasoned grains, and tangy melanges of meat or seafood and sauce. In these incarnations of traditional recipes, drawn from six continents and the seas between, salads take on many roles, from first course to main course to luncheon dish to dessert. Naturally, freshness of ingredients is everything–whether they are gathered from the garden, harvested from the field, or culled from the sea. And as every cook knows, assembling a salad for the perfect balance of color and texture, taste and aroma calls on a chef's visual arts side. The result: Culinary compositions that tantalize the taste buds while they delight the eye.

≈

The Back Garden, detail, 1850/60, Adolph von Menzel, German; oil on canvas, 18⅞ x 26¼ in. (48 x 68 cm). Founders Society Purchase, Robert H. Tannahill Foundation Fund and Mr. and Mrs. Allan Shelden III Fund (1991.172).

African Salad

2 heads ruffled green lettuce, crisped in the refrigerator

8 ounces black olives, sliced

8 ounces green olives, sliced

2 cups (1 pint) cherry tomatoes, sliced

½ cup walnuts, chopped

½ cup sunflower seeds, roasted

1 cup slivered almonds

½ cup dried figs, sliced

1 cup dates, chopped

2 firm bananas, sliced

DRESSING

¾ cup sugar

2 teaspoons dry mustard

2 teaspoons salt

⅔ cup vinegar

3 tablespoons onion juice

2 cups vegetable oil

3 tablespoons poppy seeds

Prepare dressing first: Mix sugar, mustard, salt, vinegar, onion juice, and vegetable oil together in a blender, adding oil last. Blend until thick. Stir in poppy seeds. Set aside. This dressing will keep for a long time in the refrigerator.

Break the lettuce into pieces and place in large bowl. Add olives, tomatoes, walnuts, sunflower seeds, almonds, figs, and dates; toss gently. Add desired amount of dressing and toss again. Just before serving, slice and add bananas. Toss again and serve.

SERVES 12–15

Emily Turner

❧

Kola Nut Box, 19th century, Benin, Nigeria; wood, metal, top: 4¼ x 4¼ x 14 in. (10.8 x 12.1 x 35.6 cm), bottom: 4⅞ x 4½ x 11 in. (12.4 x 11.4 x 27.9 cm). Gift of Mr. Solomon Maizel (80.112).

Barley Salad

6 beef bouillon cubes

6 cups water

1 cup pearled barley

1 cup carrots, slivered or
   grated

½ cup pine nuts

¼ cup green onions, chopped

1 red or green pepper, finely
   diced

romaine lettuce

parsley to garnish

DRESSING

4 tablespoons red wine
   vinegar

4 tablespoons olive oil

¼ teaspoon dry mustard

1 teaspoon garlic powder

¼ teaspoon white pepper

In large pot of boiling water, add bouillon cubes; when dissolved, add barley. Cover and simmer approximately 45 minutes or until soft. Drain and cool. Mix together with carrots, pine nuts, green onions, and pepper; set aside.

Combine dressing ingredients and pour half over salad. Toss and chill until serving time.

To serve, toss again, adding remaining dressing. Arrange in a bowl lined with romaine lettuce; garnish with parsley. Best when served at room temperature.

SERVES 4–6   *Jo-Anne Weingarden*

Broccoli Salad

1 cup mayonnaise

¼ cup sugar

3 tablespoons cider vinegar

2 bunches fresh broccoli florets

1 bunch green onions,
   chopped

¼ cup toasted almonds

7 slices cooked bacon,
   crumbled

1 cup raisins

Mix mayonnaise, sugar, and cider vinegar together; set aside.

Pour boiling water over the broccoli in a strainer. This makes it bright green. Mix broccoli, onions, almonds, bacon, and raisins; toss with dressing.

SERVES 10–12

Lucie Kelly

Achaemenid Court Servant with Covered Tray, 5th century B.C., Persian; limestone, 21½ x 11½ in. (54.6 x 29.2 cm), Gift of Lillian Henkel Haass (31.340).

North Shore Chicken Salad

4 cups cooked wild rice, cooked in chicken stock according to directions on package

juice of ½ lemon

1 whole boneless, skinless chicken breast, cooked and cubed

3 green onions, sliced, including tops

½ red pepper, diced

2 ounces peapods, blanched and sliced into 1-inch pieces

1 can water chestnuts, sliced

1 or 2 avocados, cut in medium-size pieces

1 cup toasted pecan halves

DRESSING

2 large cloves of garlic, minced

1 tablespoon Dijon mustard

½ teaspoon salt

¼ teaspoon sugar

¼ teaspoon pepper

¼ cup rice wine vinegar

¼ cup vegetable oil

Combine all ingredients for dressing in food processor. Set aside.

Toss warm rice and lemon juice and let cool. Add chicken, onions, and red pepper, and toss with dressing. Cover and refrigerate at least 2 hours or overnight.

Just before serving, add pea pods, water chestnuts, avocados, and pecans. Toss gently and serve over lettuce.

SERVES 4

Helen McKnight

Marinated Brussels Sprouts, Squash, and Tomato Salad

1 pound fresh Brussels sprouts, trimmed and rinsed

1½ pounds zucchini or yellow summer squash

¼ cup scallions, thinly sliced

1 pound cherry tomatoes, cut in half and seeded

1 bunch red-tipped leaf lettuce

MARINADE

1 cup salad oil

¼ cup lemon juice

¼ cup white wine vinegar

1½ teaspoons garlic, finely minced

1½ teaspoons salt

1 teaspoon sugar

½ teaspoon dry mustard

¼ teaspoon crushed hot red pepper flakes

Mix ingredients for marinade together in a bowl large enough to accommodate all the vegetables.

Bring a large pot of salted water to a rolling boil. Drop Brussels sprouts into the boiling water and cook uncovered 3–5 minutes, until barely tender. Drain into a colander and rinse thoroughly with ice cold water to stop the cooking and set the color. Slice each sprout lengthwise into 3 or 4 slices. Slice the zucchini or squash into similar-sized pieces. Combine all vegetables, except the tomatoes, with the marinade and toss thoroughly. Cover and refrigerate 1 hour. Add cherry tomatoes just before serving.

Line a serving platter with red-tipped leaf lettuce and spoon the salad vegetables onto the leaves in an attractive mound.

This salad has become a tradition at holiday time in our family. It is particularly nice with roast beef or goose.

SERVES 8–10

Linda Wells

Confetti Bean Salad

1 19-ounce can white kidney
    beans (cannellini), drained
1 15-ounce can red kidney
    beans, drained
1 15-ounce can black beans,
    drained
1 stalk celery, chopped
1 tablespoon onion, finely
    chopped
¼ cup green or red pepper,
    chopped
curly leaf lettuce

DRESSING

3 tablespoons olive oil
2 tablespoons red wine vinegar
1 small clove garlic, crushed
⅛ teaspoon basil
⅛ teaspoon parsley, chopped
salt and pepper to taste

Combine white, red, and black beans with celery, onion, and green or red pepper.

Blend olive oil, vinegar, garlic, and spices with whisk; add to bean mixture. Serve over curly lettuce.

SERVES 6–8

Pat Williams

Dried Cherry and Blue Cheese Salad

2 tablespoons dried cherries
2 tablespoons walnut pieces
blue cheese to taste
mixed greens

DRESSING

¼ cup white wine vinegar
¾ cup walnut oil
1 teaspoon Dijon mustard
salt and pepper

Combine all ingredients for dressing, mix well and set aside. To assemble, place mixed greens on plates and add dried cherries and walnut pieces; crumble blue cheese over each plate and drizzle with dressing.

You may also toss the lettuce with the dressing before placing on salad plates, then complete toppings.

Pat Wasson

French Carrot Salad

1½ pounds carrots, julienned

3 tablespoons lemon juice

2 teaspoons Dijon mustard

½ teaspoon sugar

½ cup olive oil

salt and pepper

5 green onions, minced

⅓ cup parsley, minced

red leaf lettuce

In 1 quart boiling water, blanch carrots for 2 minutes. Drain and set aside. Combine lemon juice, Dijon mustard, sugar, olive oil, salt, and pepper and pour over warm carrots. Toss with green onions and parsley. Cover and let sit 2 hours, or refrigerate and use the next day at room temperature. Serve over bed of red leaf lettuce.

SERVES 4–6

Maureen D'Avanzo

Napa Oriental Salad

1 large or 2 small heads
   Napa cabbages

6 large green onions,
   chopped

¾ stick butter

2 packages Ramen noodles,
   broken into bite size before
   cooking

⅓ cup sesame seeds

2½ ounces slivered almonds

DRESSING

1 cup oil

½ cup sugar

2 tablespoons soy sauce

½ cup cider vinegar

½ teaspoon pepper

Chop cabbage and onions into bite-size pieces and chill. Melt butter in skillet and sauté raw noodles, sesame seeds, and almonds over low heat until golden brown. Drain and set aside. Just before serving, combine cabbage and onions with noodles, sesame seeds, and almonds. Whisk dressing ingredients together and pour over salad to taste. It may not be necessary to use all the dressing.

SERVES 6–8

Ruth Lefkowitz

French and Italian Salad

1 head red-tipped leaf lettuce

1 head endive

8 slices of French baguette, cut
 ½-inch thick

4 tablespoons unsalted butter

1 8-ounce roll of goat cheese

¾ cup shredded radicchio

¾ cup fennel, thinly sliced

½ cup parsley or watercress,
 cut up

8 tablespoons walnuts,
 chopped

DRESSING

1 tablespoon wine vinegar

6 tablespoons olive oil

½ teaspoon salt

pepper to taste

Preheat oven to 400° F.

Rinse and dry leaf lettuce and endive.

Butter bread slices and toast in oven until golden. Put a slice of goat cheese on top of toast and heat in oven for 5 minutes until hot.

Arrange three lettuce and three endive leaves on each plate. Top with 1½ tablespoons each of shredded radicchio and sliced fennel; sprinkle with parsley or watercress.

Whisk together dressing ingredients and sprinkle over greens.

Before serving, place a slice of baguette on top of each salad and sprinkle each plate with 1 tablespoon chopped walnuts.

SERVES 8

Alison Jones

Goat Cheese Pasta Salad

8 ounces fusilli

8 tablespoons olive oil

4 tablespoons sherry wine
vinegar

2 tablespoons balsamic or red
wine vinegar

¼ teaspoon crushed red pepper

¼ teaspoon salt

4 tomatoes, seeded and
chopped

4 green onions, chopped

18 Kalamata olives, chopped

4 ounces salami, cubed

4 ounces goat cheese, crumbled

½ cup basil, snipped

Cook pasta according to package directions, drain. Toss pasta with two tablespoons olive oil and refrigerate until cool. Combine vinegars, red pepper, and salt and whisk in remaining olive oil. Pour over pasta; add tomatoes, onions, olives, and salami. Toss to coat. Add goat cheese and basil and toss again. Adjust seasoning. Serve on lettuce-lined platter or individual plates.

SERVES 8

Helen McKnight

Tomato Salad

3 tablespoons olive oil

2 teaspoons balsamic vinegar

salt and pepper to taste

8 sundried tomatoes, packed
in oil

1 pint cherry tomatoes, halved

2 tablespoons fresh basil,
chopped

1 large garlic clove, minced

4 leaves of red leaf lettuce

4 whole basil leaves

Whisk the oil and vinegar together and add salt and pepper to taste. Combine sundried and cherry tomatoes, chopped basil, and garlic in a mixing bowl. Pour dressing over the tomatoes and toss. Marinate at least 2 hours before serving. Divide tomatoes into four portions. Serve individually on a leaf of red lettuce and top each with a whole basil leaf.

SERVES 4

Maureen D'Avanzo

Roasted Pepper and Green Bean Salad

1 or 2 large red sweet peppers

¾ pound fresh green beans,
   stem ends trimmed

1 tablespoon Dijon mustard

1 tablespoon red wine vinegar

4 tablespoons olive oil

¼ teaspoon ground cumin

½ cup red onion, finely
   chopped

2 tablespoons parsley or basil,
   chopped

salt and freshly ground pepper
   to taste

Roast peppers; remove skins and cut into thin strips lengthwise. Set aside.

Bring a large pot of water to boil; add green beans and cook until just tender, about 3–5 minutes. Drain and refresh under cold water. Drain well. Pat dry and place in large bowl.

Put mustard and vinegar in a mixing bowl. Start beating with a wire whisk and gradually add oil. Add cumin, salt and pepper to taste. Tossing thoroughly, combine the beans, peppers, onion, and parsley with the dressing; salt and pepper again to taste. Marinate overnight.

SERVES 4–6

The Cookbook Committee

Berry Picking, ca. 1880; unknown artist, hand-tinted albumen print, 7⅝ x 10¼ in.

(19.4 x 26 cm). Collection of the Detroit Institute of Arts (x1989.11678).

Couscous and Spinach Salad

1 10-ounce box couscous

⅔ cup olive oil

1 bag fresh spinach

juice of 1 lemon

3 garlic cloves, finely chopped

3 green onions, chopped

1 pint cherry tomatoes

salt and pepper

fresh mint (optional)

Cook couscous according to directions on package. When it is done, immediately fluff with a fork and toss in a few tablespoons of olive oil (this process will prevent the couscous from clumping together). Place couscous in a shallow pan to cool. Wash spinach, remove stems and wilted leaves. Dry and set aside. Make dressing, combining remaining olive oil and lemon juice.

In a large serving bowl, toss together the spinach and couscous. Add dressing and toss again. Add garlic, green onions, and tomatoes. Toss and season to taste with salt and pepper. The addition of fresh mint leaves makes for an appealing variation.

SERVES 10

Carl Bunin

Double Cup, 19th/20th century, Suku, Zaire; wood, 5¼ x 4 x 4 in. (8.5 x 10.2 x 10.2 cm). Gift of Mourtala Diop (1992.299).

Wild Rice Salad with Walnuts and Feta Cheese

2 stalks celery, minced

½ cup parsley, chopped

4 green onions, minced

1 cup toasted walnuts

1 cup feta cheese, crumbled

½ cup sliced pimento-stuffed
 olives

1 cup herbed vinaigrette

4 cups cooked, cold wild rice
 (2 cups raw)

tomatos wedges for garnish

HERBED VINAIGRETTE

1 tablespoon fresh lemon juice

3 tablespoons wine or cider
 vinegar

1 clove garlic, minced

½ teaspoon dry mustard

1 teaspoon Dijon mustard

¼ teaspoon dried tarragon

¼ teaspoon basil

¼ teaspoon oregano

¼ teaspoon rosemary

1 teaspoon tamari or soy sauce

1 tablespoon Parmesan cheese
 (or more to taste)

¾ cup extra virgin olive oil

Mix all the salad ingredients together in a large mixing bowl. Set aside. In a small bowl, mix all ingredients for vinaigrette. Toss vinaigrette with rice mixture. Best if made the day before and left to marinate in the refrigerator. Garnish with tomato wedges and serve.

SERVES 6–8

Martha Collins

Wild Rice Salad

1 cup wild rice, uncooked
2¾ cups chicken stock
2¾ cups water
1 cup toasted, sliced pecans
1 cup currants or raisins
   (currants are preferable)
rind of 1 orange, grated
10 ounces frozen tiny peas,
   thawed
¼ cup vegetable (not olive) oil
⅓ cup fresh orange juice
salt and freshly ground pepper
   to taste

Rinse rice. Combine chicken stock and water and bring to a boil. Add rice and simmer uncovered for 35 minutes. Drain and combine rice with remaining ingredients. Mix thoroughly. Let stand 2 hours before serving.

Variation: Salad may also be mixed with diced, precooked chicken (roasted or poached) or duckling.

SERVES 4–6

The Cookbook Committee

Mustard Vinaigrette Salad Dressing

1 clove garlic
¼ teaspoon salad herbs
⅛ teaspoon tarragon
¼ teaspoon salt
¼ teaspoon sugar
2 tablespoons Dijon mustard
¾ cup extra virgin olive oil
3 teaspoons fresh lemon juice
5 teaspoons white vinegar

Put garlic and herbs in food processor and process until finely chopped. Add remaining ingredients and process until smooth.

A refreshing dressing for all types of lettuce and vegetable salads.

MAKES 1 CUP

Kathleen McCarroll, M.D.

Tropical Salad

2 heads romaine lettuce

1 head Bibb lettuce

1 papaya, peeled and sliced,
   reserving 2 tablespoons of
   seeds, discarding rest

1 large avocado, peeled and
   sliced

1 mango, peeled and sliced
   (optional)

DRESSING

½ cup sugar

2 teaspoons salt

½ teaspoon dry mustard

½ cup white wine vinegar

½ cup olive oil

½ cup onion, chopped

1 tablespoon fresh papaya
   seeds

Wash lettuce and tear into bite-size pieces. Refrigerate overnight to crisp.

Prepare dressing by placing all ingredients, except seeds, into processor or blender and mix. Add seeds and process again, only until seeds are size of coarse ground pepper. Before serving, place lettuce in large bowl. Add papaya, avocado, and mango to greens and toss gently with the dressing.

SERVES 10

Viola Hadjiyanis

***Double-Walled Ewer in the Form of
a Rooster*, late 12th/early 13th century,
Kashan, Iran; ceramic, 10⅝ x 5½ in.
(27 x 14 cm). Founders Society Purchase
with funds from Founders Junior
Council, Henry Ford II Fund, Benson
and Edith Ford Fund, J. Lawrence
Buell, Jr., Fund (1989.34).**

Sandwich Pickles

1 quart *Vlasic kosher dill*
  pickles, whole
1¾ *cup sugar*
¾ *cup cider vinegar*
2 *tablespoons pickling spice*

Drain pickles and slice into rounds. Put back in jar. In a saucepan, place sugar, vinegar, and pickling spice. Heat to boil. Pour over pickles and seal. Let sit 2 days at room temperature. Store in the refrigerator.

The Cookbook Committee

Pickle Stand, ca. 1755, Bow Factory, England; soft-paste porcelain with bone-ash, polychrome enamel decoration, height 15½ in. (34.3 cm). Founders Society Purchase with funds from Linda and John Axe, Maureen and Jerry P. D'Avanzo, Mr. and Mrs. John L. Booth II, Mary Kay and Keith Crain, Cynthia and Edsel Ford, Mr. and Mrs. Roger Fridholm, Reginald and Anne Harnett, Gerhardt and Rebecca Hein, Jean and Joe Hudson, Mr. and Mrs. Richard Janes, Mrs. Wilber Hadley Mack, Richard and Jane Manoogian, Donald and Marilyn Ross, Susan and David Thoms, Patricia and Ted Wasson, and Robert Welchli (1999.22).

Bagna Cauda Sauce-Dressing

2 tablespoons shallots, minced

1½ teaspoons garlic, minced

6 anchovy fillets

4 tablespoons red wine
  vinegar

1 teaspoon lemon juice

2 tablespoons Parmesan
  cheese, grated

¼ teaspoon salt

⅛ teaspoon pepper

1 cup olive oil

Put all ingredients, except olive oil, in processor or blender and process until anchovies are completely smooth. Slowly add olive oil and mix until creamy. If sauce thickens to mayonnaise consistency, add 1 or 2 tablespoons water.

Dressing will keep in refrigerator for a week, but will congeal and should be removed an hour or so before using. This is good on pasta primavera hot or cold, in pasta salads, or used as an eggless version of Caesar salad dressing.

Isabel Blanchard

Carrot Relish

1 pound carrots (about 6),
  peeled

1 clove garlic, minced

1 tablespoon crystallized
  ginger, minced

juice of 2 lemons

½ teaspoon cumin

½ teaspoon paprika

2 tablespoons olive oil

salt and pepper to taste

½ cup parsley, minced

In an uncovered pan with water, cook carrots until tender, 15–30 minutes. Drain. Slice carrots in rounds, ¼-inch thick.

Mix garlic, ginger, lemon juice, cumin, paprika, olive oil, and salt and pepper to taste. Pour over carrots and toss. Sprinkle with parsley before serving.

Diana Leventer

PASTA, RICE, EGG, AND CHEESE DISHES

*G*rains as trade goods, grains as offerings–and of course, grains as the basis for marvelous meals... The recipes that follow pay homage to the possibilities presented by these simplest and most abundant of ingredients. For millennia, grains, eggs, and cheese–grouped on an unadorned table or stone slab, or heaped on a groaning harvest board alongside game and other foods–symbolized the bounty of the earth and the cycle of life. These dishes, adapted from traditional recipes of the Mediterranean and the Americas, showcase the unique blend of textures and tastes that made them so beloved by the Old World and the New. Delicious on their own, they can also be combined with other treats, as taste and appetite dictate.

≈

Fusilli with Bacon and Onion Sauce

1 tablespoon virgin olive oil

½ onion, chopped

2 cloves garlic, chopped

6 fresh basil leaves or

   1 teaspoon dried

red pepper flakes to taste

3 ounces tomato paste

¼–½ pound bacon, cooked,

   drained, and crumbled

8 ounces fusilli

Asiago or Parmesan cheese

In olive oil, sauté onion until translucent. Add garlic, basil, and red pepper flakes; mix well. Sauté 1 minute. Stir in tomato paste and add bacon. Turn off heat.

Cook pasta according to directions and drain. Place in a bowl and pour the sauce over the pasta, mixing lightly. Sprinkle with cheese and serve.

MAKES 2 LARGE OR 4 MEDIUM PORTIONS

Shell Hensleigh

Fettuccini with Chicken and Spinach

2 bags spinach

¼ teaspoon nutmeg

4 large chicken breast halves,

   skinned, boned, and juli-

   enned

4 tablespoons butter

1 15½-ounce can Italian

   tomatoes

1 cup heavy cream

salt and pepper

8 ounces fettuccini

⅓ cup Parmesan cheese

Wash and stem the spinach. After shaking off most of the water, place spinach in a large saucepan over high heat. Cover and steam in its own moisture for about 3 minutes, shaking the pan occasionally. Drain, chop, season with nutmeg, and set aside.

Quickly sauté chicken in butter; remove and set aside. In the same skillet, heat tomatoes and cream until slightly thickened. Season with salt and pepper. Add chicken and spinach to the sauce and heat. Cook fettuccini according to the directions and drain. Serve the chicken and spinach sauce over the fettuccini. Serve Parmesan cheese on the side.

SERVES 6–8

Dianne Cornell

Linguine with Chicken and Asparagus

1 pound skinless, boneless
  chicken breasts

1 pound fresh asparagus,
  peeled and cut on the
  diagonal into 1-inch pieces.

¾ pound linguine or fettuccini

2 tablespoons butter

salt and pepper to taste

3 tablespoons shallots, finely
  chopped

1 cup heavy cream

1 dried hot red pepper,
  crumbled

⅛ teaspoon nutmeg, freshly
  grated

¼ pound Gorgonzola cheese,
  broken into small pieces

2 tablespoons chopped, fresh
  tarragon or ½ teaspoon
  dried

½ cup Parmesan cheese

**Dinner Plate from Service for Twelve,
1972/73, Beatrice Wood, American;
glazed earthenware, 10 in. (25.4 cm).
Gift of Garth Clark and Mark del
Vecchio (1987.64). Reprinted with
permission from the Happy Valley
Foundation, Ojai, California.**

Cut chicken into small strips. Drop the asparagus into boiling water; return to a boil. Drain immediately and set aside. Cook the pasta, drain, and set aside. Melt the butter in large saucepan. Add chicken and cook briskly until just done, stirring to separate. Add salt and pepper. Remove the chicken and set aside. Add asparagus to the pan and stir. Add shallots and cook for 30 seconds. Add cream, hot pepper, and nutmeg. Stir Gorgonzola cheese into cream mixture until melted. Return chicken to cream mixture and add the tarragon. Adjust seasoning. Add pasta to sauce and toss well. Serve with Parmesan cheese.

SERVES 4–6

Nancy Rivard Shaw

Chicken and Pasta Sauté

8 ounces pasta bowties or sea
  shells

2 tablespoons olive oil

1 pound boneless chicken
  breasts, cut into small cubes

2 garlic cloves, minced

1 carrot, julienned

½ red bell pepper, cut in thin
  strips

2 green onions, chopped

1½ teaspoons Herbs de
  Provence

¼ pound small pea pods,
  strings removed

¼ cup dry white wine

1 cup low fat evaporated milk

salt and pepper to taste

Cook pasta according to directions, drain, and keep warm. Heat 1 tablespoon olive oil in large sauté pan until hot. Add cubed chicken breast and sauté for 5 minutes. Remove chicken from pan and set aside. Add remaining olive oil and garlic to pan; heat slightly and add carrots, red peppers, green onion, and Herbs de Provence. Sauté for 5 minutes. Add pea pods and wine, simmering hard for several minutes and stirring until wine is reduced and almost evaporated. Add evaporated milk, simmering hard for approximately 5 minutes until reduced. Add reserved chicken and hot, cooked pasta to vegetable mixture and stir. Add salt and pepper to taste.

SERVES 6

Mary Ann Zinn

Tripod Bowl, Late Toltec, Mexico; terracotta with slip decorations, 7⅛ x 6¼ in. (18.1 x 15.9 cm). Gift of Dr. and Mrs. Irving F. Burton (72.274).

Vegetable Tortilla Lasagna

2 tablespoons vegetable oil

1 large zucchini, cut crosswise
    into ¼-inch thick slices

¾ cup frozen corn, thawed

¼ cup ricotta cheese

1¼ cups Monterey Jack cheese,
    grated

½ teaspoon ground cumin

salt and pepper to taste

1 cup tomato salsa

1 7-ounce jar roasted red
    peppers, drained and patted
    dry

2 tablespoons fresh coriander
    (or 2 teaspoons dried)

6 6-inch corn tortillas

lime wedges

Preheat oven to 500° F.

Brush 2 shallow baking pans with oil. In one pan, arrange zucchini in single layer. Put corn in second pan. Sprinkle both with salt and pepper and roast in oven about 5 minutes. Stir corn. Continue roasting about 5 minutes more, or until lightly browned.

While vegetables are roasting, in a small bowl, stir together ricotta cheese, one cup Monterey Jack, cumin, and salt and pepper to taste.

Drain salsa in a fine sieve set over a bowl for 3 seconds—do not press on solids. Lightly grease an 8½ x 4½ x 3-inch loaf pan. Trim tortillas into six 5 x 3¾-inch rectangles. Cover bottom of loaf pan with two tortillas, overlapping them in the middle, and spread ¼ cup salsa over tortillas. Top with half of cheese mixture, half zucchini, half peppers, half corn, and half coriander. Make another layer of tortillas and ½ cup salsa. Top with remaining cheese mixture, vegetables, and coriander. Make another layer of tortillas; add remaining salsa and Monterey Jack cheese. Cover lasagna with foil and bake in middle of oven 12 minutes or until heated through and cheese is melted. Let stand covered 5 minutes before serving.

Serve with lime wedges as an accompaniment.

SERVES 2 AS A MAIN COURSE, 4 AS A FIRST COURSE

Racquel Ross

Seven Vegetable Couscous

1½ cups couscous

3 cups boiling chicken or vegetable stock

1 tablespoon butter

1 teaspoon turmeric

1 teaspoon salt

2 tablespoons vegetable oil

2 medium onions, chopped

2 large carrots, sliced

1 cup cabbage, shredded

1 medium turnip, peeled and
diced

1 medium yellow squash or
zucchini, diced

1 15½-ounce can chickpeas
(garbanzo beans), drained

1 teaspoon cinnamon

½ teaspoon each ground
cumin, coriander, and salt

⅓ cup raisins

¼ cup parsley, chopped

⅓ cup sliced almonds, toasted

Combine the couscous and boiling stock in bowl. Cover and let stand until stock is absorbed, about 15 minutes. Fluff with a fork; stir in butter, turmeric, and salt. Cover and set aside.

Heat the vegetable oil in a large, deep, heavy pan. Add onions and sauté over moderate heat until translucent. Stir in carrots, cabbage, turnip, and squash or zucchini. Cook until crisp tender. Add chick-peas, cinnamon, cumin, coriander, salt, and raisins. Cover and heat. Vegetables should be tender but firm.

Arrange couscous around the edge of a large, flat serving dish. Put vegetables in the center. Sprinkle with parsley and almonds.

SERVES 8

Gail and Charles McGee

Etruscan Rice

¾ pound Italian sausages

1 large green pepper, cut in
  strips

1 large onion, sliced

1½ cups cooked ham, cubed

1 7-ounce package saffron
  (yellow) rice

2½ cups water

1 3½-ounce jar roasted
  pimentos

Skin and crumble the sausages; brown the meat in a skillet. Add peppers and onions and sauté until softened. Add ham, rice, and water. Bring to a boil; cover and reduce to simmer for 20–25 minutes. Cut pimentos into strips; stir into rice mixture. Heat 1 minute before serving.

SERVES 6–8

Helen Oak

Syrian Rice

½ cup orzo

½ cup butter

2 cups washed brown or white
  rice

4 cups salted water

In a heavy pot, brown orzo in melted butter. Add rice and water. Bring to a boil; cover and turn down heat. Simmer and cook 10 minutes or until all water is absorbed. Set lid ajar to let steam escape. Fluff with a fork when done. This can be prepared ahead and reheated in the microwave.

SERVES 10–12

Josephine Machour

Breakfast Egg and Sausage Casserole

1 pound roll pork sausage

8 eggs

10 slices bread, cubed

3 cups milk

2 cups cheddar cheese,
   shredded

2 cups fresh mushrooms, sliced

1 10-ounce package frozen cut
   asparagus, thawed and
   drained

2 tablespoons flour

1 tablespoon dry mustard

2 teaspoons basil

1 teaspoon salt

Preheated oven to 350° F.

In a large skillet, brown the sausage and drain. In a large bowl, beat eggs and add all ingredients, mixing well. Spoon into greased glass 13 x 9-inch baking dish. Cover and refrigerate for 8 hours or overnight. Bake 60–70 minutes or until knife inserted near the center comes out clean.

SERVES 10   *Joseph Samulowicz*

Barley with Mushrooms

1 cup quick barley, uncooked

8 tablespoons butter at room
   temperature

1 pound mushrooms, sliced

1 clove garlic, minced

3 tablespoons parsley, chopped

½ teaspoon salt

⅛ teaspoon pepper

¼ teaspoon marjoram

¼ cup water

Preheat oven to 350° F.

Prepare barley according to directions on box and drain. In heavy pan, melt four tablespoons butter and add mushrooms, garlic, parsley, salt, pepper, and marjoram. Sauté 5 minutes. Combine mushroom mixture, barley, remaining butter, and ¼ cup water. Put in a greased mold, place in pan of hot water, and bake for 30 minutes. This dish can be prepared ahead.

SERVES 6–8

Mrs. H. Alexander McDonald

Northwoods Garlic Frittata

10 eggs

¾ cup milk

½ cup Parmesan cheese,
  grated

3 tablespoons butter

5 cloves fresh garlic, minced

½ cup onion, chopped

1 green pepper, chopped

½ red pepper, chopped

1 to 4 ounces Polish or garlic
  sausage, chopped

4 or 5 large potatoes,
  shredded or chopped,
  or 16 ounces frozen hash
  browns

4 ounces cheddar cheese,
  shredded

Beat together eggs, milk, and Parmesan cheese and set aside. In a large skillet, melt butter. Sauté garlic, onion, peppers, and sausage. Add potatoes and sauté until tender—about 5 minutes. Pour egg mixture into skillet and cook until eggs are almost set. Sprinkle cheddar cheese on top of frittata. Place pan 6 inches from broiler and heat until top is bubbly and slightly browned. Cut into wedges and serve.

SERVES 10

Sandra Moers

Ceremonial Bowl, early 20th century, Cameroon; terracotta, 20 x 11 in. (50.8 x 27.9 cm). Founders Society Purchase, Prepaid Gifts Fund, African Art Fund, and Edsel and Eleanor Ford Fund (80.60).

Bundt Noodle Kugel

½ cup butter, melted

¾ cup dark brown sugar

1 cup pecan pieces

4 eggs, beaten

1 cup applesauce

1 teaspoon salt

½ teaspoon cinnamon

⅔ cup sugar

1 cup sour cream

1 16-ounce package wide
noodles, cooked and drained

Pour ¼ cup melted butter into greased bundt pan. Sprinkle brown sugar over the butter and mix together. Top with nuts and set aside. In a large bowl, beat eggs and add applesauce, salt, cinnamon, sugar, sour cream, and remaining butter. Mix thoroughly with noodles. Spoon into pan over nut mixture. Bake at 350° F for 1 hour. Let stand at room temperature for 10 minutes before inverting on serving plate.

SERVES 12

Lois Singer

Cottage Cheese Pancakes

4 eggs, separated

1 cup cottage cheese (low-fat
can be used)

½ cup flour

1½ teaspoons sugar

2 teaspoons vanilla

Beat egg whites until stiff. Combine remaining ingredients and fold into egg whites. Heat a buttered frying pan or griddle. Drop mixture by large spoonfuls and cook on both sides until golden. Serve with heated maple syrup or sliced fruit.

SERVES 2

Dede Feldman

A Banquet in the Open Air, early 4th century A.D., Roman; marble, glass, and terracotta, 25¼ x 25¼ in. (59.1 x 59.1 cm).
Founders Society Purchase, Sarah Bacon Hill Fund (54.492).

Noodle Kugel

1 teaspoon salt

1 teaspoon vegetable oil

8 ounces wide noodles

¼ pound butter

3 ounces cream cheese

1 pound small curd cottage
cheese (low-fat can be used)

¾ cup sour cream (low-fat can
be used)

¾ teaspoon salt

1 teaspoon vanilla

3 eggs

1 10-ounce can crushed
pineapple, undrained

½ cup golden raisins

TOPPING

1½ cups corn flakes, crushed

1–2 teaspoons cinnamon

1–2 tablespoons brown sugar

butter

Bring 2 quarts water to a boil. Add one teaspoon salt and vegetable oil. Add noodles and cook 6–8 minutes. Drain. Cut butter into slices and add to drained noodles. Mix until butter is melted and set mixture aside. Beat cream cheese until soft and add cottage cheese, sour cream, salt, and vanilla. Beat eggs and add to mixture. Mix in pineapple and raisins and add all to noodles. Stir well. Pour into greased 9 x 13-inch pan. Combine corn flakes, cinnamon, and brown sugar and place on top of kugel mixture. Dot with butter and bake in preheated 350º F oven for 1–1¼ hours. Top should be brown.

SERVES 12

Lois Lesser

Bowl, 9th century, Abbasid Dynasty, Iraq; earthenware with overglaze luster decoration, 2½ x 8¼ in. (6.3 x 21 cm). Founders Society Purchase, Dr. and Mrs. Arthur Bloom Fund, Mary Martin Semmes Fund, Edna Burian Skelton Fund, and Hill Memorial Fund (1994.80).

Vegetable Cheese Bake

4 tablespoons butter or olive
  oil

3 cups French or sourdough
  bread, cubed, crusts removed

1 cup celery, chopped

1 cup sweet red pepper,
  chopped

1 cup scallions, chopped
  (green tops included)

1 cup fresh mushrooms,
  quartered

1 clove garlic, crushed, or
  ½ teaspoon garlic powder
  (optional)

1½ cups cooked corn (off the
  cob) or 15 ounces canned
  corn, drained

4 eggs

2 cups milk

10 ounces extra sharp cheddar
  cheese, grated

¼ teaspoon dry mustard

¼ teaspoon ground pepper

1 teaspoon parsley

paprika

Preheat oven to 350° F.

Butter a 2-quart casserole with 1 tablespoon butter or oil. Add bread cubes and set aside. In a large skillet, sauté celery, peppers, scallions, mushrooms, and garlic in 3 tablespoons butter or oil until translucent; add the corn. In the 2-quart bowl, whisk eggs. Add milk, cheese, mustard, pepper, and parsley. Toss vegetable mix into bread; add egg mixture, tossing until bread is coated. Dust with paprika, cover casserole, and refrigerate overnight. Bake uncovered for 1 hour until bubbly and slightly crusty. Let casserole sit 5 minutes before serving.

SERVES 6–8

Phyllis McLean

VEGETABLES AND LEGUMES

Freed forever from the role of humble side dish, vegetables and legumes now lay claim to the chef's full attention. And why not? Chopped, grilled, pureed, or served au naturel, vegetables are now available in a variety of colors, textures, and flavors from the corner market or gourmet store, giving cooks a whole new palette with which to work. As artists from the Dutch still life painters to contemporary realists recognized, the shapes of vegetables and legumes are in themselves delights. But in these recipes, luscious forms spiced and combined with other taste-tempters are matched by new twists on traditional flavors from the East—Eastern Europe, East Asia, and the East Coast of the United States.

~

Vegetable Stall, detail, 1665, Quiryn Gerritsz van Brekelenkam, Dutch; paint on wood panel; 18⅛ x 14⅞ in. (46.7 x 37.8 cm). Gift of James E. Scripps (89.52).

Red Cabbage Confit

8 cups thinly sliced red
  cabbage (about 2 pounds)
1 large onion, thinly sliced
1 bay leaf
¼ teaspoon dried thyme
4 dried allspice berries or
  ¼ teaspoon allspice
2 garlic cloves, unpeeled and
  crushed
fresh cracked black pepper to
  taste
2 tablespoons olive oil
1 apple, peeled and grated
1 cup dry red wine
¼ cup red wine vinegar
2 tablespoons sugar
1 cup water
½ cup Michigan cherries,
  dried currants, or dried or
  fresh blueberries

Blanch the cabbage for 2 minutes in a large pot of boiling salted water; drain and remove to a separate dish. Wipe the pot and add oil. Cook the onion, bay leaf, thyme, allspice, garlic, and pepper over very low heat, stirring regularly until the onion is softened. Return blanched cabbage to pot and add the apple, wine, vinegar, sugar, and water. Bring to a boil, then cover and simmer for 30 to 35 minutes or until cabbage is tender. Add fruit and simmer uncovered, stirring occasionally, for 10 minutes or until most of the liquid has evaporated. Discard the bay leaf, allspice berries, and garlic. Season further with pepper, if desired.

Can be prepared in advance and reheated.

SERVES 8–12

Graham W. J. Beal
Director, The Detroit Institute of Arts

Sautéed Cabbage with Fruit

6 tablespoons unsalted butter

5 ounces dried pears, coarsely chopped

4 shallots, sliced

1 small garlic clove, minced

1 cup clear chicken broth

3 pounds savory or other green cabbage, finely shredded

⅔ cup dried cherries, sweet or sour

¼ cup balsamic vinegar

2 tablespoons parsley, minced

½ teaspoon salt

¼ teaspoon finely ground pepper

In a large Dutch oven, melt butter over medium heat. Add pears, shallots, and garlic; sauté 15 minutes or until very soft but not brown. Add chicken broth, cabbage, cherries, and vinegar and mix. Cook 15 minutes or until cabbage is tender, tossing often. Turn heat to high; bring to a boil for an additional 15 minutes or until liquid is mostly evaporated, stirring frequently. Remove from heat; add parsley and seasonings.

SERVES 8

Eileen Kozloff

Tureen in the Form of a Cabbage, with Matching Platter, ca. 1777/80 Niderviller Manufactory, French; faience (tin-glazed earthenware), 7¾ x 12 x 14 in. (19.7 x 35.6 x 35.6 cm). Bequest of Bernard Savage Reilly (1999.86.A–C).

Carrot Tzimmis (Pudding)

3 pounds carrots, peeled and
  grated or chopped in food
  processor
1 large sweet potato, peeled
  and grated or chopped in
  food processor
¼ cup chopped onion
¼ teaspoon salt
¼ teaspoon pepper
½ teaspoon cinnamon
¼ cup white sugar
½ cup light brown sugar
¼ pound butter

KNAIDEL (DUMPLING)

2 cups flour
¼ teaspoon salt
¼ teaspoon pepper
½ teaspoon cinnamon
3 tablespoons butter, softened
¼ cup chopped onion
2 egg yolks
5–6 tablespoons hot water
3 tablespoons brown sugar,
  reserved

For the tzimmis: Mix together and put in large pot. Cover with cold water. Bring to a boil. While mixture is cooking, prepare knaidel.

For the knaidel: Mix all ingredients, except brown sugar. Make into 1 or 2 firm balls of dough.

Place knaidel in center of pot with carrot mixture. Fold carrots over to cover knaidel. Sprinkle with brown sugar. Cook, partially covered, for about ½ hour on medium heat. Remove and place in moderate over (350° F). Keep covered for 1 hour. Then uncover. Break up knaidel with a spoon and mix into the carrot mixture. Cook uncovered for another 2 hours or until all juice is evaporated and carrots are golden brown. Blend carrots and knaidel with spoon.

May be made a day ahead and refrigerated. Before serving, dot with butter and warm in oven. Additional brown sugar may be added if mixture is not sweet enough.

SERVES 10–12

Leah Drachler

Flan des Carottes

CRUST

1 cup flour

½ teaspoon salt

⅓ cup shortening, chilled

1 tablespoon butter

2 tablespoons water

FILLING

1¾ pounds new carrots, peeled

2 tablespoons water

½ cup butter

½ cup onion, finely chopped

1 teaspoon sugar

⅛ teaspoon salt

½ cup cream or half-and-half

1 teaspoon dill weed

salt and pepper to taste

Preheat oven to 450° F.

Mix flour and salt together. Cut in shortening and butter until it has the grain of cornmeal. Sprinkle dough with water and blend in lightly until you can gather dough into a ball. Chill. Roll out to fit 10-inch pie pan and prick dough with a fork. Bake 10–12 minutes or until lightly brown. Reduce oven temperature to 425° F.

Cook ½ to ¾ cup of sliced carrots in water until just tender. Set aside. Coarsely chop remaining carrots. Combine water and butter in pan over medium heat; add coarsely chopped carrots, onions, sugar, and salt. Cook, stirring frequently, until liquid is absorbed and carrots are just tender. Purée the carrot mixture in a blender or food processor. Blend in cream, dill, salt, and pepper. Fill pie shell with carrot mixture. Decorate with sliced carrots. Bake in oven for 15–20 minutes.

SERVES 6–8

Mary Jane Bostick

Corn Pudding

16 ounces cream-style corn

½ cup flour

2 cups whole milk

4 tablespoons sugar (optional)

4 tablespoons melted butter

salt and pepper to taste

4 eggs, beaten

Preheat oven to 350° F.

Combine corn, flour, milk, sugar, butter, salt, and pepper. Fold into beaten eggs. Bake in greased flat 1½-quart dish for 45 minutes.

SERVES 6

Star O'Brien

Eggplant Chiaroscuro

3 tablespoons oil

1 medium onion, sliced

2 tablespoons fresh ginger,
   diced

1 tablespoon garlic, diced

1 medium-large eggplant,
   peeled and cubed

1 pound tofu, cubed

1 cup mushrooms, sliced

1 cup brown rice, cooked
   according to directions
   on package

snap peas or asparagus
   cooked crisp tender
   (optional)

SAUCE

6 tablespoons soy sauce

3 tablespoons sherry

2 teaspoons sugar

1 tablespoon vinegar

water to make 1½ cups

Sauté onion in oil until soft but not brown. Add ginger and garlic. Cook 3–4 minutes, stirring to prevent browning. Remove and set aside. Sauté eggplant for 15 minutes, adding extra oil if needed. Add tofu, mushrooms, and onions to eggplant and cook 5–10 minutes. Mix ingredients for sauce. Add to vegetables and continue cooking for 5–10 minutes, stirring occasionally, until eggplant is tender.

Serve on hot brown rice. Garnish with snap peas or asparagus as desired.

SERVES 6

Natalie Lederer

Eggplants, **detail, ca. 17th century, formerly attributed to Unkoku Toeki, Japanese; ink on paper, 9½ x 15⅜ in. (24.1 x 54.6 cm). Gift of Dr. and Mrs. Irving F. Burton (65.565).**

Green Bean Bundles

2 pounds green beans,
  trimmed

8 green onions, including long
  green stems

1 red pepper, cut into ¼-inch
  thick strips

½ cup butter

1 clove garlic, chopped

½ teaspoon crushed thyme

¼ teaspoon white pepper

Preheat oven to 375° F. Cook beans in salted water for 3 minutes. Remove from pot and plunge beans into ice cold water. Drain. Blanch green onions for 15 seconds. Remove and pat dry. Cut onions off stems and discard. Gather a serving-size bundle of beans. Tie onion stem around beans and knot. Place bundles in a buttered 8-inch square pan. Slip two red pepper strips under each knot and set aside. Melt butter in small pan. Sauté garlic 3 minutes; add thyme and pepper, and pour over beans. Bake 7–10 minutes until heated through.

SERVES 8

Marilyn Gushée

Spinach Casserole

1 pound fresh spinach

3 tablespoons butter

1 pound mushrooms, sliced

½ cup onion, chopped

¼ teaspoon nutmeg

salt and pepper to taste

6 ounces cream cheese, cubed

1½ cup white cheddar cheese,
  grated

1 pint box cherry tomatoes,
  halved

2–3 tablespoons Parmesan
  cheese, grated

Preheat oven to 325° F.

Cook spinach until wilted. Drain, chop, and set aside. Sauté onion and mushrooms in butter until softened. Add seasonings.

Layer in 6-cup casserole: half the spinach, all the mushroom-onion mixture, and all cream cheese cubes. Add remaining half of spinach and cover with cheddar cheese. Bake for 20 minutes. Arrange tomatoes on top of spinach. Dust with Parmesan cheese and bake 5–10 minutes more.

SERVES 4–6

Liz Kuhlman

Woman Sitting at a Table, 1924,
Pierre Bonnard, French; oil on
canvas, 31 x 15⅜ in. (78.7 x 39.7 cm).
Gift of Mr. and Mrs. Abraham L.
Bienstock (59.443). © 2000 Artists
Rights Society (ARS), New York/
ADAGP, Paris.

Spinach Ring

2 boxes frozen, chopped
   spinach
2 cups boiling, salted water
2–3 tablespoons onion, minced
   finely
4 tablespoons melted butter
2 eggs, slightly beaten
½ teaspoon salt
¼ teaspoon pepper
¼ teaspoon nutmeg
½ cup bread crumbs
carrots, cooked and buttered
toasted almonds

Preheat oven to 350° F.

Drop frozen spinach into boiling, salted water. Bring to boil again for 4–6 minutes. Drain. Add onion, butter, eggs, seasonings, and bread crumbs. Mix well and turn into well greased, 4–5 cup ring mold. Place ring mold in pan of hot water and bake until firm, approximately 30 minutes. Remove from water and allow to sit for 10 minutes before unmolding. Garnish center of ring mold with carrots. Sprinkle with toasted almonds.

SERVES 6

Elsie Golden

Roasted Sweet Potatoes

5 pounds sweet potatoes,
   washed, cut into wedges
1 large onion, sliced
olive oil
pepper
rosemary

Preheat oven to 400° F.

Place potatoes and onion in a 9 x 12-inch baking dish. Drizzle olive oil over mixture and lightly toss. Season generously with pepper and rosemary. Bake 30–40 minutes or until tender.

SERVES 6–8

Jane Solomon

Pommes de Terre Gruyère or Basilic Nutmeg Potatoes

3 pounds Idaho potatoes,
   peeled and sliced ¼-inch
   thick
2 tablespoons olive oil
2 garlic cloves, minced
1½ pounds ripe tomatoes,
   peeled and diced
½ ounce fresh basil (approximately 24–30 leaves),
   chopped
1 grated whole nutmeg
1 pint cream
salt and pepper to taste
8 stalks celery, sliced
juice of one lemon
½ pound grated Gruyère
   cheese

Preheat oven to 375° F.

Boil potatoes in salt water until not quite soft. Sauté garlic in olive oil–do not brown. Add tomatoes and basil, then stir in nutmeg. Continue to stir for 3 minutes. Add cream, salt, and pepper and heat for additional 5 minutes.

In a small saucepan, cover celery with water and lemon juice. Cook until half the liquid has evaporated.

Oil or butter a 9 x 12-inch baking dish. Place potatoes in a single overlapping layer. Cover evenly with celery mixture and half of the tomato mixture. Sprinkle with half the cheese; add the remaining tomatoes and top with remaining cheese. Bake for 1 hour until cheese is golden brown.

SERVES 10–12

Dirk Bakker

Gadrooned Vessel with Tripod Parrot Feet, 200 B.C./A.D. 500, Colima, Mexico; ceramic with red slip, 8½ x 12½ in. (21.5 x 31.7). Bequest of W. Hawkins Ferry (1988.196.1–.2).

Cranberry Squash

1 ½ cups raw cranberries,
   halved

¼ cup dry sherry

2 eggs

3 tablespoons butter, melted

½ cup sugar

½ teaspoon salt

¼ teaspoon pepper

1 teaspoon nutmeg, grated

4 cups mashed, cooked squash
   (4 pounds fresh butternut
   squash or 2–3 packages
   frozen squash, thawed)

Preheat oven to 400° F.

Marinate cranberries in sherry approximately 15 minutes. In a large bowl, beat eggs. Add butter, sugar, salt, pepper, and nutmeg. Stir in prepared squash, cranberries, and sherry. Pour into greased 2-quart casserole and bake, uncovered, for 30 minutes.

SERVES 8

Phyllis McLean

Crispy-Top Vegetable Casserole

½ cup boiling water

2 cups small carrot sticks

2 cups zucchini slices, ¼-inch
   wide

1½ teaspoons salt

6 tablespoons butter

2 teaspoons flour

1½ cups half and half

2 chicken bouillon cubes,
   crumbled

½ teaspoon prepared mustard

½ teaspoon dill weed

dash of nutmeg

dash of pepper

1 8-ounce can tiny onions,
   drained

1 cup soft bread crumbs

½ cup cheddar cheese, grated

½ cup walnuts, coarsely
   chopped

Preheat 375° F.

Bring saucepan of water to boil; add carrots, zucchini, and salt and return to boil. Cover and cook 5–10 minutes. Drain well.

Melt two tablespoons butter in a saucepan and stir in flour. Gradually stir in half-and-half. Add bouillon, mustard, and ¼ teaspoon of the dill weed, nutmeg, and pepper. Cook, stirring until mixture comes to a full boil. Remove from heat. Add carrots, zucchini, and onions and turn mixture into a greased 7-cup baking dish.

Melt remaining butter and toss with crumbs, cheese, walnuts, and remaining ¼ teaspoon dill weed. Heap over vegetable mixture. Bake, uncovered, 25–30 minutes, until topping is browned and sauce bubbles at edges.

SERVES 6

Elsie Golden

Vegetable Medley

2 tablespoons oil

2 medium onions, sliced thin

1½ teaspoons turmeric

1 teaspoon ground ginger

1½ pounds medium-size mush-
    rooms, quartered

4 teaspoons lemon juice

1 teaspoon salt

4 medium-size fresh tomatoes,
    cut into wedges

2 10-ounce packages frozen
    petite peas, defrosted

Heat oil in a large skillet. Sauté onions with turmeric and ginger on low to medium heat until translucent. Add mushrooms, lemon juice, and salt and continue to sauté until cooked. This may be prepared ahead of time and kept at room temperature.

Just before serving, warm the onion-mushroom mixture; place tomatoes in skillet and sprinkle peas over top. Cover and cook 2 minutes.

SERVES 10–12

Miriam Kostantin

Vidalia Onions in Madeira Cream

8 tablespoons butter

4 large Vidalia onions, peeled,
    sliced ¼-inch thick

½ cup Madeira

salt and pepper to taste

¼ cup heavy cream

¼ cup parsley, finely chopped

Melt butter in a wide, heavy skillet. Add onion slices and turn to coat. Cover and cook over medium to low heat 25–35 minutes, turning occasionally. Uncover pan, increase heat slightly, and stir in Madeira. Stirring frequently, cook until Madeira evaporates, about 2 minutes. Season to taste. Stir in cream and parsley. Bring to boil, stirring. Reduce heat and simmer for 1 minute.

SERVES 6

Margie Gillis

FRESHWATER FISH AND SEAFOOD

a *mainstay for coastal residents, a luxury for inland dwellers... no matter where fish and seafood are served, the wealth of flavors, textures and forms found in these fruits of lake and sea will elevate mere meals to memorable occasions. Likewise, artists from time immemorial have celebrated fish and those who make their living culling—and eating—food from the sea. Whether it's a simply etched Greek platter, bearing the graceful outlines of a scaled fish, or a painting of a Dutch interior, replete with citizens dining on oysters by flickering candlelight, the central role played by the water's bounty—in art and life—is abundantly clear. That role, and variety, is reflected in the recipes here... hearty fish stews and baked loaves, delicate casseroles, and spicy fish fillets.*

≈

Baked Catfish

1 catfish, whole or fillets,
  cleaned with cold water
seasoning salt
garlic powder
pepper to taste
1 whole lemon
1–2 onions, cut in strips
1–2 bell peppers, cut in strips

Preheat oven to 350° F. Place fish on a piece of heavy-duty foil large enough to wrap all the fish. Season with salt, garlic powder, and pepper; squeeze lemon juice over fish. Slice the lemon and place slices around fish. Spread onions and peppers on fish and enclose the fish in the foil by tightening the ends and top. Place foil packet in pan and bake 30–60 minutes, depending on size of fish. Check and turn fish once. Transfer to platter and serve hot.

SERVES 4

Clara Ellington

Fish Loaf

3 slices bread (challah or egg
  bread is best), crust removed
½ cup skim milk
3 eggs or 1 egg plus 2 egg
  whites, lightly beaten

2 pounds ground, chopped
  fillet of pickerel or whitefish
  or combination of the two
1½ teaspoons salt
1 teaspoon sugar

½ teaspoon pepper
1 large onion, very finely
  grated
red horseradish

Preheat oven to 375° F. Soak bread in milk combined with eggs. Add all other ingredients and blend thoroughly. Place mixture in a well-buttered 10 x 5 x 3-inch loaf pan and bake for 1 hour or until brown on top. Cool, remove from pan, and refrigerate. Slice and serve with red horseradish.

SERVES 12–14

Lila Silverman

Thirteen Bean Bouillabaisse

1 14-ounce package 13 Bean
 Bouillabaisse Bean Cuisine
 Soup Mix
2 tablespoons olive oil
1 cup carrots, chopped
1 cup celery, chopped
1 cup onion, chopped
8 cups water
2 cups Clamato juice
2 bottles clam juice
1 14-ounce can crushed
 tomatoes

3 large cloves garlic, crushed
salt, pepper, and Tabasco
 sauce to taste
1 pound seafood or fish
 (scallops, shrimp, cod,
 whitefish)

Soak the soup mix package of beans 6–8 hours, using enough water to cover well. Drain. In a large pot, sauté vegetables in oil until soft. Add other ingredients except seafood or fish. Simmer until beans are tender, about 3½ hours. (Soup freezes well at this point.) 10–15 minutes before serving, add seafood or fish and simmer until cooked. Serve hot.

SERVES 8   *Ruth Waldfogel*

Island Grilled Halibut

6 halibut steaks 1 inch thick

MARINADE

2 cloves garlic, peeled and
 sliced
¼ teaspoon white pepper
2 tablespoons sugar
⅓ cup soy sauce
6 tablespoons corn oil
3 green onions, chopped
1 tablespoon sesame seeds

Combine all the marinade ingredients and pour over halibut in a shallow pan. Cover and marinate in refrigerator overnight. Place steaks on a preheated grill. Cook 7 minutes on each side or until the fish flakes easily.

SERVES 6   *Arden Poole*

Grilled Salmon Fillets

2 pounds salmon fillets

8 tablespoons butter, melted

1 teaspoon onion powder

½ teaspoon pepper

1 teaspoon salt

1 teaspoon garlic powder

½ teaspoon Worcestershire
   sauce

½ teaspoon paprika

1 teaspoon Cajun seasoning
   (optional)

Preheat barbeque grill on high. Spray a large piece of heavy-duty foil with cooking oil spray. Mix together the butter and seasonings; brush on fish. Wrap fish in foil, skin side down, and grill until well done, about 30 minutes, turning every 5 minutes.

SERVES 4

Lenore Dorfman

Salmon au Poivre

¾ pound center cut salmon
   fillet, cut into 2 pieces

4 teaspoons pepper, coarsely
   ground

2 teaspoons olive oil

MARINADE

2 tablespoons soy sauce

1 clove garlic, mashed

2 teaspoons lemon juice

2 tablespoons olive oil

1 teaspoon sugar

Mix marinade ingredients in a plastic bag and add salmon. Seal bag and refrigerate 30 minutes. Remove salmon from marinade; pat dry and press two teaspoons pepper onto each side of each fillet piece. In a skillet, cook the fish in two teaspoons olive oil for approximately 2 minutes, or until it flakes, turning once.

SERVES 2

Racquel Ross

Lime Marinated Salmon with Cilantro Butter

2 pounds salmon fillet cut into
   5-ounce portions

MARINADE

⅓ cup lime juice

2 cups onion, chopped

2 teaspoons garlic, minced

2 tablespoons jalapeño
   peppers, chopped

1 bunch cilantro

2 tablespoons red chili honey

¼ cup olive oil

1 teaspoon salt

CILANTRO BUTTER

¼ pound unsalted butter,
   softened

½ cup cilantro, chopped

1 tablespoon fresh ginger,
   grated

2 teaspoons lime juice

Combine marinade ingredients in a food processor and pulse for 30 seconds. Pour the marinade into a ceramic dish; place the salmon in the marinade and coat. Marinate for 1–2 hours. Remove the salmon and season with salt and pepper; place on a hot grill and cook for 2–3 minutes per side, depending on thickness. Top each fillet with a teaspoon of cilantro butter.

For the cilantro butter, combine all ingredients in a food processor and pulse until smooth. Serve at room temperature.

This butter is also delicious served with grilled chicken breast.

SERVES 6

Maureen D'Avanzo

Bowl with Fish, 11th–15th century, Byzantine; terracotta with white slip under pale yellow glaze, 10⅝ x 5⅜ in. (27 x 8.9 cm). Founders Society Purchase, William H. Murphy Fund (71.125).

Mama's Sweet-and-Sour Trout

5 pounds whole trout cut into
   2-inch slices

salt

white vinegar to cover fish
   (approximately 4–6 cups)

3 tablespoons granulated
   sugar

1 large yellow onion, sliced

2 quarts cold water

½ cup dark brown sugar

2 large lemons, thinly sliced

1 cup dark, seedless raisins

6 whole allspice berries

6 dried bay leaves

¼ teaspoon cinnamon

2 gingersnaps

Place a single layer of fish in a glass or ceramic bowl; lightly salt and refrigerate for 1½ hours. Wash salt off and return to bowl; cover with white vinegar and let marinate overnight.

In a frying pan, melt the white sugar and add the sliced onion; cook until golden brown. Transfer to a large pot. Add 2 quarts cold water, brown sugar, sliced lemons, raisins, and the spices. Bring to a simmer, cook ½ hour, and skim. Taste for seasoning. Carefully add fish and simmer for ½ hour longer. Remove from heat and skim.

Mash the gingersnaps in a bowl with enough fish stock from the pot to make a thin paste. Pour the mixture over the fish, shaking the pot gently to evenly distribute. Remove fish and gingersnap mixture to a glass or ceramic bowl and refrigerate. Serve cold.

SERVES 10

Sylvia Dunitz

The Oyster Breakfast, ca. 1650–1660, Hendrik van der Burch, Dutch; oil on panel, 15 x 15 in. (58.1 x 55 cm). City of Detroit Purchase (28.56).

Cold Whitefish with Dill and Tomato-Cucumber Relish

vegetable oil

4½ pounds whitefish cut into 2
    fillets (fatty portions
    trimmed along center and
    flap edges)

3 cups fresh dill, coarsely
    chopped

1 medium onion, coarsely
    chopped

1 teaspoon kosher salt

¼ teaspoon ground pepper

6 tablespoons white vinegar

RELISH

4 cups diced, peeled, seeded
    cucumber

2 pounds plum tomatoes,
    seeded and chopped

½ cup fresh dill, chopped

¼ cup white vinegar

4 teaspoons kosher salt

fresh dill sprigs

Line heavy baking sheet with foil and brush with oil. Arrange fish on foil, skin side down. Finely chop dill and onion in a processor. Sprinkle each fillet with salt and pepper. Press dill and onion mixture firmly on top of fish. Pour vinegar evenly over the fish. Cover and chill overnight, basting occasionally with juices.

Position rack in center of oven and preheat to 375° F. Uncover fish and bake until just cooked through, about 25 minutes. Let stand at room temperature 30 minutes. Cover and chill at least 2 hours and up to 2 days.

For relish, combine first five ingredients in a medium bowl. Let stand 3 hours, stirring occasionally. Season with pepper.

Scrape most of dill off fish. Cut crosswise into serving portions, trimming neatly. Slide spatula under each serving, separating flesh from skin. Arrange fish on plates. Drain relish and spoon over fish. Garnish with dill sprigs.

SERVES 4–6

Rosalind Grand

Herb Shrimp and Feta Casserole

2 large eggs

1 cup evaporated milk

1 cup plain yogurt

8 ounces feta cheese, crumbled

⅓ pound Swiss cheese,
    shredded

⅓ cup fresh parsley, chopped

1 teaspoon dried basil

1 teaspoon dried oregano

4 cloves garlic, minced

½ pound angel hair pasta,
    cooked

1 16-ounce jar chunky salsa

1 pound medium-sized raw
    shrimp, peeled

½ pound mozzarella cheese,
    shredded

Preheat oven to 350° F.

Coat bottom and sides of an 8 x 12-inch baking dish with cooking spray. In a bowl, blend eggs, milk, yogurt, feta and Swiss cheeses, parsley, basil, oregano, and garlic. Set aside. Spread half of pasta over bottom of baking dish. Cover with salsa and add half of shrimp. Spread remaining pasta over shrimp. Pour and spread egg mixture over pasta. Add remaining shrimp and top with Mozzarella cheese. Bake 30 minutes. Remove from oven and let stand 10 minutes before serving.

SERVES 12

Helen McKnight

Bent Corner Bowl, ca. 1830, Kaigani Haida culture, Alaska; wood, 8½ x 7½ in. (21.5 x 19 cm). Founders Society Purchase, New Endowment Fund, Henry Ford II Fund, Henry E. and Consuelo S. Wenger Foundation Fund (1988.12).

POULTRY DISHES

From ancient days until our own, poultry has ruled the roost, offering flavor and economy. And in the case of chicken, familiarity has bred thousands of ways to prepare it. The recipes in these pages reflect poultry's international popularity: a sherried poulet in the French tradition, as succulent as any in a still life display; a Greek Island version of what might have been Homer's original feast; casserolled pollo with a Latin accent; and poultry with Asian, Italian and red-hot American flavors. Put out the plates (fine china or paper, as the occasion demands) and prepare to dish out that promised—and oh so promising—chicken found in every pot.

≈

Artichoke Chicken

¼ cup butter

2½–3 pounds chicken, cut into
   serving pieces

1 clove garlic, chopped

2 tablespoons onion, chopped

1 tablespoon tomato paste

2 tablespoons flour

1½ cups chicken broth

2 tablespoons sherry (optional)

1 teaspoon dried tarragon

1 can artichoke hearts, cut up

salt and pepper to taste

In a skillet, heat the butter. Add the chicken and brown on all sides on high heat. Remove the chicken from the skillet and keep it warm. Reduce temperature to low and add the garlic and onion to the skillet; cook 3 minutes. Add the tomato paste and flour and combine until you have made a smooth paste. Stir in the chicken broth (and optional sherry). When the mixture comes to a boil, return the chicken to the pan; add tarragon, artichoke hearts, salt, and pepper. Cover and simmer slowly 45–50 minutes.

SERVES 4

Margie Fitzsimmons

Curried Lemon Chicken

6 chicken breast halves and
   6 thighs and/or drumsticks

1 or 2 garlic cloves

salt and pepper to taste

½ lemon

¼ pound butter

2½ tablespoons curry powder

¾ cup prepared mustard

1 cup honey

1 teaspoon soy sauce

Rub garlic on chicken, and season with salt and pepper to taste. Arrange chicken in a 9 x 13-inch baking dish; squeeze lemon over chicken. Melt butter and stir in curry powder. Blend in the mustard, honey, and soy sauce and pour mixture over chicken. Cover with foil and refrigerate overnight.

Bring chicken to room temperature and bake for 1 hour in a preheated 350° F oven, basting at intervals.

SERVES 8

Martha Beechler

Cold Curried Chicken

6 cups cooked, cubed chicken

¾ cup flaked, unsweetened
   coconut

1½ cups celery, sliced

1½ cups golden raisins

1½ cups dry roasted, unsalted
   peanuts

1½ cups green peppers,
   chopped

6 tablespoons chutney,
   chopped

DRESSING

¾ cup yogurt

¾ cup mayonnaise

¾ cup sour cream

1 tablespoon lemon juice

1 tablespoon curry powder

6 tablespoons onion,
   chopped

¾ teaspoon salt

Combine all salad ingredients thoroughly. Prepare dressing by whisking the listed ingredients together. Present the salad and dressing in separate serving dishes, or, toss the salad with enough dressing to lightly coat and bind together. Serve remaining dressing on the side.

SERVES 12–16

Helen McKnight

Tray, ca. 1885, Christopher Dresser, English; brass and copper, 12⅜ x ¾ in. (51.5 x 1.8 cm). Founders Society Purchase, European Sculpture and Decorative Arts General Fund (1991.10).

Birds Following a Plough, 1933, Ethel Spowers, Australian; linoleum cut printed in color on oriental paper, 8 x 12¼ in. (20.5 x 31.1 cm). Founders Society Purchase, John S. Newberry Fund (1997.58).

Chicken San Miguel

6 chicken breasts, skinned,
  boned, and cut in half

3 cups chicken broth (more as
  needed), divided

¼ cup butter

2 sprigs fresh tarragon or
  1 teaspoon dried

3 tablespoons instant flour
  (this is a granular flour
  which is often used as a
  thickener)

1 cup half-and-half

1 egg yolk, lightly beaten

1 teaspoon lemon juice

salt and pepper to taste

1 8-ounce jar or can of artichoke bottoms

1 pound mushroom caps,
  mixed domestic and wild

1 sweet red bell pepper

1 poblano pepper, fresh or
  canned, julienned

½ cup pine nuts, toasted in
  oven until lightly browned

Preheat oven to 300° F.

In a pot, poach the chicken in two cups of simmering broth for 20 minutes, just until tender. Arrange breasts in a large baking dish.

In a pan, heat the butter on low heat with the tarragon; blend flour into butter, straining out tarragon if sprigs are used. Add remaining broth and half-and-half. Cook, stirring constantly, until the sauce thickens, adding more broth if needed. Stir a spoonful of the hot sauce into the egg yolk and return both to the remaining sauce, cooking over very low heat until cooked through. Add the lemon juice and season to taste. Pour the sauce over the chicken, covering completely, and garnish with the artichoke bottoms. (This may be prepared up to this point and refrigerated.)

Heat in oven 10–15 minutes. Meanwhile, sauté the mushrooms and peppers in a little oil for 3–4 minutes. Garnish the chicken with the mushrooms and peppers. Sprinkle with pine nuts and serve.

SERVES 6

Joy Emery

The Mayor's Favorite Chicken (French Chicken in Orange Sherry Sauce)

3 chicken breasts, split (2½–3 pounds)

½ teaspoon salt

1 medium-sized onion, sliced

¼ cup green pepper, chopped

1 cup mushrooms, sliced

SAUCE

1 cup orange juice

¼ cup dry sherry

½ cup water

1 tablespoon brown sugar, firmly packed

1 teaspoon salt

¼ teaspoon pepper

1 teaspoon grated orange rind

1 tablespoon flour

2 teaspoons parsley, chopped

paprika

1 orange, peeled and sliced

Preheat oven to 350° F. Quickly brown the chicken breasts in a pan. Place chicken breasts in a shallow 3-cup baking dish. Sprinkle with salt. Add onion, green pepper, and mushrooms.

For the sauce, combine orange juice, sherry, water, brown sugar, salt, pepper, orange rind, and flour in a small saucepan. Cook over medium heat, stirring constantly, until sauce thickens and bubbles; add parsley. Pour over chicken.

Bake uncovered in moderate oven 45 minutes or until chicken is tender. Baste several times. To serve, sprinkle with paprika and garnish with orange slices.

SERVES 6

The Honorable Trudy DunCombe Archer

Easy Chicken

6 skinless, boneless chicken
   breast halves
¼ cup white wine
½ cup Dijon mustard
1 cup soft bread crumbs
½ cup Parmesan cheese
¼ cup parsley, finely chopped

Preheat oven to 375° F.

Combine wine and mustard and set aside. Combine thoroughly the bread crumbs, cheese, and parsley. Dip chicken in wine/mustard mixture; roll in crumb mixture. Place on greased cookie sheet and bake 30 minutes until tender.

SERVES 6

The Cookbook Committee

Chicken Imperial

1 whole chicken cut into
   quarters or eighths
½ cup orange juice
¼ cup soy sauce
¼ cup ketchup
¼ cup honey
1 teaspoon dried basil
¼ teaspoon pepper

Preheat oven to 350° F.

Place the chicken in shallow baking pan after rinsing and drying thoroughly. Mix remaining ingredients and pour over chicken to coat all pieces. Bake uncovered 1 hour.

SERVES 4

Lois Singer

Tray with Design of Cranes in Flight, 17th century, Ryukyu Islands, Okinawa; red lacquer on wood with inlaid mother-of-pearl and incised gold decoration, 11¾ x 11¾ in. (29.8 x 29.8 cm). Founders Society Purchase with funds from Mrs. Howard J. Stoddard and Mr. and Mrs. Stanford C. Stoddard (1987.32).

Greek Chicken with Feta Cheese

8 ounces feta cheese, sliced

6 skinless, boneless, chicken
   breasts, pounded

2 tablespoons olive oil

4 medium onions, thinly sliced

2 large garlic cloves, minced

1 28-ounce can tomatoes, with
   liquid, coarsely chopped

1 teaspoon dried basil

freshly ground black pepper to
   taste

Place feta cheese in a bowl with enough cold water to cover, and set it aside.

Heat one tablespoon oil in a covered, heavy skillet. Brown the chicken breasts over moderate heat, turning them several times. Transfer chicken to a platter.

Add one tablespoon oil to skillet, along with sliced onions. Cook onions over moderately low heat about 5 minutes, stirring constantly. Add garlic and cook for another 5 minutes or until onions start to brown.

Add tomatoes and basil, stirring mixture to combine ingredients.

Place chicken breasts on the sauce; sprinkle ingredients with a generous amount of pepper. Cover skillet and bring ingredients to a boil; reduce the heat to medium-low and simmer chicken for 30 minutes.

Remove feta cheese from water and arrange slices on top of chicken. Cover skillet and cook chicken for another 15 minutes or until cheese is melted.

Can be served over pasta or rice.

SERVES 6

Joyce Harding

Coupe, ca. 1878, Veuve Ferdinand Duvinage, Fench; silvered bronze, ivory marquetry, copper alloy, exotic woods, 15.9 x 46.4 cm (6¼ x 18¼ in.). Founders Society Purchase, Joseph M. de Grimme Memorial Fund (1995.82).

Turkey Breast on Barbecue

6 pounds skinless, boneless
   turkey breast
2 large shallots, chopped
½ cup orange juice
3 tablespoons olive oil

2 tablespoons rosemary
2 tablespoons balsamic
   vinegar
4 teaspoons grated orange peel
1 tablespoon honey

⅛ teaspoon dried red pepper
   flakes
pepper and garlic powder to
   taste

Flatten meat to 1 inch thick. Combine all other ingredients and marinate turkey in mixture for 6–12 hours. Grill over medium heat approximately 16 minutes on each side or until done, watching carefully. Baste with mixture several times.

SERVES 12

Mary Ann Simon

MAIN COURSE MEATS

*R*oasted, stewed, fricasseed, grilled, or ground–meat dishes are more than a culinary centerpiece. Holding mirrors to our moods, they conjure memories of past celebrations and crown our present triumphs. Inspiring great art–think of Flemish genre paintings, the table groaning with roasted duck, chicken and pig, or Chardin's still lifes of choice cuts on a platter–they also have inspired a range of recipes, from the most complicated blends of tastes and textures, to that epitome of fast food for home, the burger. Our own recipes explore select aspects of meat's bounty–lamb, pork, and beef dishes formally prepped and attired, or bound for the casual barbeque grill.

≈

Still Life with Fruit, Vegetables, and Dead Game, detail, ca. 1635–37, Frans Snyders, Flemish; oil on canvas, 65⅛ x 78¼ in. (166.1 x 200 cm). Founders Society Purchase, Acquisitions Fund (78.44).

Sweet-and-Sour Beef Stew with Dried Cherries

3 tablespoons all-purpose flour

1¼ teaspoons salt

½ teaspoon ground allspice

½ teaspoon ground cinnamon

½ teaspoon pepper

2 pounds boneless beef chuck, cut into 1-inch cubes

4 tablespoons vegetable oil

2 large onions, thinly sliced

1 cup dried, pitted, sour cherries or dried apricots, quartered

2 tablespoons sugar

2 tablespoons red wine vinegar

2 tablespoons water

1 cup dry red wine

1 cup beef stock or canned broth

½ pound button mushrooms, trimmed and quartered

Preheat oven to 350° F with rack in center position.

Combine flour, salt, allspice, cinnamon, and pepper in a large plastic bag. Add beef to bag and toss, coating pieces evenly with seasoned flour. Heat one tablespoon oil in heavy skillet over medium-high heat. Add one-third of beef and cook until brown, about 5 minutes. Transfer meat to a Dutch oven, using a slotted spoon. Repeat with remaining meat in two batches, adding 1 tablespoon oil to skillet each time.

Add remaining oil to same skillet. Stirring frequently, add onions and cherries (or apricots) and cook until onions are soft and light brown, about 12 minutes. Mix in sugar, vinegar, and water. Increase heat to high and cook until onions brown, stirring frequently, about 8 minutes.

Add onion mixture to beef in Dutch oven. Mix in wine, stock, and mushrooms; cover tightly and bake until beef is tender, about 2 hours 15 minutes, uncovering stew during last 2 minutes if liquid is too thin. Serve or cover and refrigerate. Stew can be prepared 2 days ahead. Bring to room temperature first and reheat over low heat.

SERVES 6

Michelle Morouse

One Great Meat Loaf

---

2 pounds lean, ground sirloin

2 eggs, lightly beaten

18 ounces natural mild salsa

6 ounces seasoned bread
  crumbs

Preheat oven to 425° F.

Knead ingredients gently with one hand in the following order: meat, egg, salsa, and bread crumbs. Form a large loaf and place it in a baking dish with the meat loaf not touching the sides. Bake 1 hour and 20 minutes or until the meat is thoroughly cooked.

Please note that the salsa will become spicier in the cooking process. A medium salsa may be used–but not for the faint-hearted–as it will, after the cooking process, become quite sharp.

SERVES 6

Earl R. Jacobs

Park Avenue Bones

12 beef ribs cut into single
   portions
fresh garlic, minced
salt and pepper to taste
¾ cup red wine vinegar
¾ cup Dijon mustard
¾–1 cup seasoned bread
   crumbs
melted butter (optional)
parsley

Preheat oven to 350º F. Season ribs with garlic, salt, and pepper. Roast ribs in oven for approximately 1 hour or until tender. Remove from pan and drain off fat. Generously sprinkle red wine vinegar over ribs and marinate for several hours. Smear Dijon mustard completely over each rib and roll in seasoned bread crumbs. Set aside until ready to serve. Before serving, put under hot broiler for 1–2 minutes to crisp. If desired, drizzle melted butter over ribs. Garnish with parsley and serve immediately.

SERVES 6–8

Linda Dresner

Party Leg of Lamb

8 pounds leg of lamb
2 cloves garlic
1 teaspoon salt
¼ teaspoon ground pepper
2 tablespoons olive oil
1 teaspoon dried thyme
1 teaspoon dried marjoram
1 teaspoon dried rosemary
2 tablespoons flour
1 cup white wine
1 cup water

Preheat oven to 325º F. Place lamb in roasting pan. In small bowl, crush garlic and add salt, pepper, and oil. Mix well. Rub over surface of lamb. In same bowl, mix together thyme, marjoram, rosemary, and flour. Press on surface of lamb. Pour wine and water into pan bottom. Roast in oven 20–25 minutes per pound, or until meat thermometer registers 140º F for rare, 160º F for medium, or 170º F for well-done, as desired. Baste frequently with wine and water mixture. Remove roast to heated platter and let it rest 15 minutes before carving. Skim fat from pan drippings and make gravy or serve as sauce over sliced lamb.

SERVES 8

Gary and Linda Assarian

Zebra Mesa, 1987, José Chardiet, American; glass, height 40 in. (101.6 cm). Gift of the Jack A. and Aviva Robinson Collection (1996.86).

Barbecued Leg of Lamb

6–8 pounds butterflied leg of
lamb, all fat removed

MARINADE

½ cup olive oil
¼ cup lemon juice
1 teaspoon salt

1 teaspoon marjoram
1 teaspoon thyme
½ teaspoon pepper
3 cloves garlic, minced
½ cup purple onions, chopped
½ cup parsley, snipped

Combine all marinade ingredients and pour over meat in ceramic or glass dish. Cover and let marinate overnight. Grill over hot coals to desired doneness.

SERVES 8–10

Liz Kuhlman

Country Lamb Bake

4 lamb shoulder chops
4 crushed garlic cloves, additional as needed
⅛ teaspoon marjoram
⅛ teaspoon thyme
⅛ teaspoon oregano
2 tablespoons flour
2 tablespoons olive oil
2 large white onions, sliced
2 large tomatoes, sliced
1 cup white wine
2 bay leaves
3 baking potatoes, peeled and sliced

Preheat oven to 275° F.

Rub lamb with combined garlic, marjoram, thyme, and oregano. Dust with flour and brown the lamb in olive oil. In a casserole dish, layer onion, tomato, and lamb. Add wine and enough water to go halfway up meat. Add the bay leaves and additional garlic as desired. Bring to a boil on stove top. Place casserole in oven for 3 hours. In the last ½ hour, add layers of potatoes. At this point, dish can be cooled and placed in refrigerator for later reheating.

Skim off any fat. The casserole mixture should be moist; if there is too much juice, cook down on stove. This dish can also be put under broiler just before serving.

SERVES 4

Susan Sovel

Grilled Pork Skewers with Couscous Topped with Tomato Basil Compote

1 teaspoon Dijon mustard

1 teaspoon honey

juice of 1 lemon

1 tablespoon fresh thyme
(about 4 sprigs), plus more
for garnish

salt and freshly ground pepper
to taste

2½ tablespoons olive oil, plus
more to brush on grill

2 cloves garlic, peeled and
finely chopped

1¼ pounds pork tenderloin,
trimmed and cut into 1-inch
cubes

½ medium red onion, diced
into ¼-inch pieces

½ each small zucchini and
yellow squash, diced into
¼-inch pieces

1 each red and yellow pepper,
seeded and diced into ¼-inch
pieces

1 cup dry couscous

1 cup boiling water

TOMATO BASIL COMPOTE

1½ tablespoons olive oil

2 cloves garlic, peeled and
thinly sliced

1½ pints yellow, red, and
orange pear and cherry
tomatoes, in any combination

salt and freshly ground pepper
to taste

8 large basil leaves

In a large bowl, mix Dijon mustard, honey, lemon juice, thyme, salt, pepper, 1 tablespoon oil, and half the garlic. Add the pork; cover and let stand for at least ½ hour.

Heat remaining oil in a saucepan over medium-low heat. Add remaining garlic and the onion. Cook until translucent, about 4 minutes. Add zucchini, squash, and peppers; raise heat and cook until just soft, about 5 minutes more. Add couscous and water; stir well. Turn off heat; cover and let sit for 5 minutes. Season with salt and pepper to taste.

Heat grill and brush with oil. Thread pork on skewers; season with salt and pepper. Grill on each side until done. Serve over couscous.

For compote, heat oil in a large skillet over medium-low heat. Add garlic and cook until soft and golden, about 3 minutes. Add tomatoes; season well with salt and pepper and cook, stirring often, until tomatoes are just warm and ready to burst, 3–5 minutes. Add basil and cook until just wilted, about 1 minute. Spoon compote over cooked pork skewers.

SERVES 4

The Cookbook Committee

Grilled Pork Chops with Cranberry-Peach Chutney

1¼ pounds center cut, boneless
pork chops
1 tablespoon corn oil
salt and pepper to taste

CHUTNEY

1 tablespoon olive oil
¼ cup onions, chopped
2 teaspoons fresh ginger,
minced
⅓ cup dried cranberries
2 ripe peaches, peeled and
sliced
⅓ cup fresh orange juice
1 tablespoon fresh lemon juice
2 tablespoons brown sugar
2 teaspoons cider vinegar
salt and pepper to taste

Coat the pork chops very lightly with oil, salt, and pepper. Place on hot grill and cook approximately 4 minutes on each side.

Serve pork with the chutney.

For the chutney, heat olive oil in sauce pan and sauté onions until translucent, about 4 minutes. Add ginger and sauté an additional minute. Reduce heat to low and add cranberries, peaches, orange juice, lemon juice, and brown sugar. Cook over low heat for 25 minutes until peaches are soft and cranberries are plump. Add vinegar, salt and pepper to taste.

SERVES 4

Lucie Kelly

Treille, 1996, Janet Fish, American; screenprint printed in color on wove paper; 26 x 18 in. (66 x 45.7 cm). Gift of the Graphic Arts Council (1996.251).

Fricando : Spareribs and Sausages Braised with Wine Vinegar

2½ tablespoons butter

3 carrots, finely chopped

2 onions, finely chopped

2 stalks celery, finely chopped

4 tablespoons olive oil

3 mild Italian sausages

3 pounds baby back ribs, cut
   into 2 rib sections

6 cloves

2 bay leaves

2½ tablespoons red wine
   vinegar

2 tablespoons tomato paste

1¾ cups water

4 potatoes, peeled and cut into
   8–10 pieces

salt and pepper to taste

Melt butter in heavy pot and sauté the carrots, onions, and celery until they are soft. Remove to a plate. Coat the pan with the olive oil; prick the sausages and add them to the pan along with the ribs. Sauté until brown; drain off the fat. Add cloves, bay leaves, and vinegar; raise the heat and let bubble until liquid evaporates. Add the tomato paste diluted in water. Return the vegetables to the pot; season with salt and pepper to taste; cover and cook over medium-low heat 1½–2 hours, turning the sausages and ribs every so often. You may need to add water if it gets dry. Add the potatoes and cook another ½ hour, turning them over so that they absorb the sauce and cook evenly. This dish improves in flavor when prepared the day before and reheated to serve.

SERVES 6

Carole Skau

Spoon with Head on Handle, 20th century, Senufo, Sudan; wood, 7⅜ x 2 in. (18.7 x 5.1). Bequest of Robert H. Tannahill (70.108).

Grilled Veal Chops

4–6 veal chops, 1-inch thick

½ cup olive oil

1 cup basil leaves, firmly
  packed

¼ cup lemon juice

grated peel of 1 lemon

2–3 cloves of garlic, sliced

1 tablespoon Dijon mustard

Trim chops of all fat. Combine all other ingredients and coat the chops, marinating them at room temperature 30 minutes. Cook veal chops over very hot grill for about 6 minutes per side.

SERVES 4–6

Liz Kuhlman

Veal Chops with Cream and Capers

4 veal chops

1½ tablespoons butter

1½ tablespoons vegetable oil

1½ tablespoons shallots,
  chopped

1½ cups beef stock

¼ cup sherry or Madeira

1 tablespoon lemon juice

1 cup whipping cream

1 tablespoon capers

salt and pepper to taste

In large skillet, brown chops in combined butter and oil for 6–10 minutes, depending on size. Remove chops and keep warm. Add shallots to skillet and cook until softened. Add beef stock, sherry or Madeira, lemon juice, cream, and capers. Cook down until thickened and season to taste. Pour over chops and serve.

SERVES 4

Isabel Blanchard

BREADS AND BAKED GOODS

*D*etails of a lifetime flooded back to Proust with a single nibble on his madeleine. The breads and baked goods in this section are sure to have the same effect. . . awakening forgotten memories—or forming new ones. Bread making and baking have always been viewed as symbols of tradition, and time's continuum. Artists, of course, see pastry in a different light—as round or pointed loaves whose surfaces contrast with the meat and drink on a still life table. Bread becomes the symbol of a people, a place, an attitude—Irish soda, New York rye. But no matter the ethnic origins of a loaf, the universal custom of "breaking bread" shows our shared need—and common humanity.

∾

Apple-Carrot Muffins

2 eggs

⅔ cup sugar

5 tablespoons butter

1½ cups apples, peeled and
  shredded

½ cup carrots, shredded

1 teaspoon vanilla

1¾ cups flour

1½ teaspoons baking powder

1 teaspoon baking soda

⅓–½ cup golden raisins

½ cup nuts, chopped
  (optional)

½ cup coconut (optional)

GLAZE

½ cup powdered sugar

⅓ teaspoon orange or lemon
  extract

1 teaspoon water

Preheat oven to 350° F.

Beat eggs with sugar. Add butter, apples, carrots, and vanilla and blend well. Combine separately flour, baking powder, and baking soda; add to egg mixture, mixing thoroughly. Stir in raisins, nuts, and coconut; combine well.

Spoon into 14 paper-lined muffin tins. Bake for about 30 minutes.

For glaze, mix powdered sugar, orange or lemon extract, and water to smooth consistency. Brush on hot muffins.

MAKES 14 MUFFINS

Suzanne Tushman

***Ti Weave Basket*, mid-19th century, Pomo, California; willow, sedge, redbud or bulrush, 12⅜ x 18 in. (31.4 x 45.7 cm). Founders Society Purchase, Joseph H. Parsons Fund (1994.32).**

Cranberry Sunrise Muffins

⅔ cup vegetable oil

1⅓ cup light brown sugar,
  packed firm

1 egg, room temperature

1 teaspoon vanilla

1 cup buttermilk

2½ cups flour

1 teaspoon baking soda

½ teaspoon cinnamon

1 tablespoon orange zest,
  finely minced

1¾ cups cranberries, coarsely
  chopped, or chopped frozen
  berries, not defrosted

STREUSEL TOPPING

1 tablespoon butter

⅓ cup light brown, dark
  brown, or white sugar

½ teaspoon cinnamon

½ cup walnuts, finely chopped

Preheat oven to 350° F.

In a large bowl, whisk together oil, brown sugar, and egg until oil and egg are absorbed by the sugar. Do not over beat. Blend in vanilla and buttermilk. In a separate large bowl, sift together flour, baking soda, and cinnamon. Sprinkle in orange zest and gently toss to coat. Stir flour mixture into oil mixture until liquid is absorbed. Do not over mix. Fold in cranberries. Spoon batter into 12 paper-lined muffin tins. Tins will be very full.

For topping, in small bowl, combine butter and sugar until crumbly. Stir in cinnamon and nuts. Sprinkle streusel topping evenly over each muffin.

Bake 25–30 minutes or until tester comes out clean. Remove from oven. Let sit in pan 5 minutes before removing. These freeze well.

MAKES 1 DOZEN LARGE MUFFINS

The Cookbook Committee

Lemon Bread

½ cup vegetable shortening

1¼ cups sugar

2 eggs, slightly beaten

1¼ cups all purpose flour

1 teaspoon baking powder

½ teaspoon salt

½ cup milk

½ cup (2 ounces) nuts,
  chopped

grated rind and juice of
  1 lemon, separated

Preheat over to 350° F.

In mixing bowl, cream together shortening and 1 cup sugar. Mix in eggs and set aside. Sift together flour, baking powder, and salt. Alternately add flour mixture and milk to shortening mixture, stirring constantly. Stir in nuts and lemon zest. Pour into one 9 x 5-inch or two 5 x 7-inch greased loaf pans. Bake in center of oven for 50 minutes or until cake tester comes out clean.

In a small bowl, mix together ¼ cup sugar and lemon juice. After bread is baked, poke holes in top of loaf and pour sugar-lemon juice mixture over the top. Cool in pan or on wire rack.

Leslie Lazzerin

Date Nut Bread

1 8-ounce package pitted
  dates, chopped

1 cup raisins

1 cup boiling water

1 teaspoon baking soda

¼ pound butter

1 cup sugar

2 large eggs

2 cups cake flour, sifted

2 teaspoons vanilla

Preheat oven to 325° F.

In a mixing bowl, combine dates, raisins, water, and baking soda and set aside. In another bowl, cream butter and sugar with mixer; add eggs one at a time. Mix well. Blend in flour and add vanilla; fold in date mixture. Line a 9⅝ x 5½ x 2¾-inch loaf pan with waxed paper. Pour in batter. Bake for 1 hour.

Rena Levy

The Kitchen at Piette's, Montfoucault, 1874, Camille Pissarro, French; oil on canvas, 17¼ x 21½ in. (45.1 x 54.6 cm). Bequest of Edward E. Rothman (75.31).

Mini Orange-Pepper Muffins

4 tablespoons unsalted butter, softened, plus more for greasing pans

1 tablespoon sugar

1 egg

1 tablespoon orange juice

2 scallions, finely chopped

¾ cup all-purpose flour

½ cup yellow cornmeal

½ teaspoon baking powder

½ teaspoon baking soda

½ teaspoon kosher salt

2 teaspoon grated orange zest

1½ teaspoon 5-pepper mix, coarsely ground

½ cup sour cream

Preheat oven to 375° F. Grease two miniature muffin pans and set aside. Beat butter until light. Beat in sugar and then the egg. Mix in orange juice and scallions.

In separate bowl, stir together flour, cornmeal, baking powder, baking soda, salt, orange zest, and pepper mix. Add to the butter mixture alternately with the sour cream, mixing just to combine.

Spoon the batter into the prepared pans and bake until the muffins are lightly browned and spring back when touched in the center, about 15 minutes. Serve warm or at room temperature.

MAKES 2 DOZEN MUFFINS

Judith Weiner

Irish Soda Bread

2½ cups unbleached flour

5 tablespoons sugar

1 teaspoon baking powder

5 tablespoons Butter-Flavor
   Crisco

¼ cup dried Michigan cherries
   or dried black currants

¾ cup golden raisins

1 teaspoon baking soda

¼ teaspoon salt

1 tablespoon apple cider
   vinegar

1 cup buttermilk

Preheat oven to 350° F.

In mixing bowl, combine flour, sugar, and baking powder. Cut shortening into flour mixture until it resembles small beads. Add dried cherries or currants and raisins. In a large glass or ceramic bowl, combine baking soda, salt, vinegar, and buttermilk.

With fork, mix together wet and dry ingredients and knead 4 or 5 times. Roll into ball and slightly flatten top. Place on greased, floured cookie sheet. Cut an ✕ shape into top of loaf. Put one tablespoon butter in ✕ and rub loaf with buttermilk.

Bake for 50–60 minutes. When done, loaf will be beautifully browned and when tapped, will sound hollow.

MAKES 1 LOAF

Pam Watson

Strawberry Bread

3 cups all-purpose flour

1 teaspoon baking soda

½ teaspoon salt

1 tablespoon ground
   cinnamon

2 cups sugar

3 eggs, beaten

1 cup vegetable oil

2 10-ounce packages frozen,
   sliced strawberries, thawed

Preheat oven to 350° F.

In a bowl, combine and mix well the flour, baking soda, salt, cinnamon, and sugar; set aside. Combine eggs, oil, and strawberries and add to dry ingredients; mix well.

Pour batter into 2 greased and floured loaf pans (9 x 5 x 3 inches). Bake 1 hour or until tester inserted into center comes out clean.

MAKES 2 LOAVES

Janice Sobel

Whole Wheat Apricot Bread

¾ cup water

½ cup raisins

½ cup dried apricots, cut into
  pieces

1 ½ cups whole wheat flour

½ cup brown sugar

¼ cup granulated sugar

1 teaspoon baking powder

½ teaspoon baking soda

½ teaspoon salt

2 eggs, slightly beaten

¼ cup butter, melted

1 teaspoon vanilla

½ cup walnuts, chopped

Preheat oven to 350° F.

In medium saucepan, combine water, raisins, and apricots. Bring to a boil, remove from heat and cool. Do not drain.

In large mixing bowl, stir together flour, both sugars, baking powder, baking soda, and salt. Stir in apricot mixture, eggs, butter, and vanilla. Fold in walnuts. Turn into a greased 9 x 5 x 3-inch loaf pan. Bake 40–45 minutes. Cool in pan for 10 minutes. Remove from pan and cool on rack.

This can also be baked in three 12-ounce loaf pans. Bake 35–40 minutes.

MAKES 1 LARGE OR 3 SMALL LOAVES

Gloria Baykian

DESSERTS, COOKIES, AND CONFECTIONS

*N*ewcomers to the table (relatively speaking), desserts as we know them did not become a meal's sweet end until the early 16th century, when sugar and chocolate were first combined. Hard as it is to believe that the luscious concoctions we take for granted today are so young, in culinary years, desserts certainly have made up for their late start with an abundance of recipes that must delight even those most determined to avoid such treats. Fruits, nuts, ice creams, candies. . . the list of alluring delights in these pages reminds us that our universal sweet tooth has prompted the creation of many of cuisine's true marvels. . . from un-humble pies laced with layers of sweets and spices to tortes and creams unrivaled for their flavors and textural fineness.

≈

Athanasia's Custard Cake

1 quart milk

1¼ cups sugar

⅛ teaspoon salt

½ cup farina

10 eggs, separated

¾ cup unsalted butter

1 teaspoon vanilla

¾ teaspoon cream of tartar

Preheat oven to 350° F.

In saucepan, heat milk, 1 cup sugar, and salt over low heat. Slowly add farina, stirring constantly, until mixture is smooth and thick–about 45 minutes. Remove to large bowl and cool.

Beat egg yolks with butter and remaining ¼ cup sugar until light and creamy; add vanilla. In separate bowl, beat egg whites with cream of tartar until the peaks hold but are not too dry. Fold whites into beaten egg yolks. Carefully fold the combined egg mixture into cooled farina. Pour into 9 x 13-inch greased pan and bake for 30 minutes until top is lightly brown.

Optional: Sprinkle with powdered sugar and/or cinnamon.

Cool, cut into squares, and serve.

Tula Georgeson

Tea Glasses Holder, late 19th/early 20th century, Tuareg, African; brass, silver, copper, 5¾ x 8⅛ x 2¾ in. (9.5 x 20.6 x 7 cm). Founders Society Purchase with funds from the Friends of African and African American Art, the African, Oceanic, and New World Cultures General Fund, Mr. and Mrs. Allan Shelden III Fund, and the Henry E. and Consuelo S. Wenger Foundation Fund (1994.24).

Blueberry Rhubarb Dessert

¾ cup sugar

¼ cup flour

½ teaspoon cinnamon

1 teaspoon grated lemon zest

4 cups blueberries

3 cups rhubarb, diced

TOPPING

1 cup flour

½ teaspoon cinnamon

¼ cup brown sugar

⅓ cup butter

½ cup pecans, chopped

Preheat oven to 375° F.

In a large bowl, stir together sugar, flour, cinnamon, and lemon zest. Add berries and rhubarb; mix lightly. Transfer to a shallow, ungreased, baking dish.

Mix flour, cinnamon, and brown sugar. Cut in butter with a pastry blender and add pecans. Spoon topping evenly over fruit. Bake for 35–40 minutes. Serve warm with ice cream or whipped cream.

SERVES 8

Shirley Wayburn

Chocolate Rum Torte with Chocolate Ganache

¾ cup plus 2 tablespoons flour

½ teaspoon baking powder

¼ teaspoon baking soda

½ teaspoon salt

2 ounces unsweetened chocolate, in pieces

1¼ cups sugar

1 tablespoon cocoa

⅓ cup boiling water

¾ cup unsalted butter, softened, cut in pieces

2 eggs

½ cup sour cream

1 tablespoon dark rum

Preheat oven to 325° F.

Butter bottom and sides of a 9½- or 10-inch springform pan. Cut circle of wax paper to fit bottom of pan. Butter and flour paper.

Combine flour, baking powder, baking soda, and salt in a food processor. Process for 5 seconds. Transfer to mixing bowl and set aside.

Combine chocolate, sugar, and cocoa in processor. Process for 1 minute. With motor still running, add boiling water then butter. Process for 1 minute. Add eggs and process for another minute.

Scrape down sides of processor. Add sour cream and rum and process 5 seconds. Add flour mixture and process, using 5 on/off pulses. Do not over process or batter will be thin.

Pour into prepared pan. Bake 40 minutes or until cake pulls away from sides of pan. Cool cake. Release side from pan. Invert and peel wax paper from bottom of cake; place cake right side up on plate pooled with custard sauce.

VANILLA CUSTARD SAUCE

2 cups half-and-half

⅔ cup whole milk

1 vanilla bean, split

5 egg yolks

⅔ cup sugar

dash salt

For the custard sauce, combine half-and-half and milk in sauce-pan. Scrape vanilla bean seeds into milk and add bean pod. Bring mixture just to a simmer. Cover, remove from heat, and let steep 1 hour.

Whisk egg yolks, sugar, and salt.

Bring half-and-half mixture back to a boil. Whisk a little into the egg yolks,then whisk yolks back into pan with half-and-half. Cook over low heat until custard thickens slightly and leaves a path on the back of a wooden spoon when finger is drawn across, about 8–10 minutes. Do not boil.

Cover and refrigerate until well chilled.

GANACHE

8 ounces bittersweet or semi-
  sweet chocolate

½ cup heavy cream

2 tablespoons light corn syrup

1 tablespoon dark rum

candied violets

For the ganache topping, chop chocolate in small chunks in food processor. Heat cream to boiling and pour in processor while motor is running. Add corn syrup and rum and pulse to process. Refrigerate for 10 minutes or until spreading consistency. Spread on cooled cake; decorate with candied violets.

SERVES 10–12

The Cookbook Committee

Ontario Apple Pie

¾ cup brown sugar

1½ tablespoons flour

½ teaspoon salt

1 egg, slightly beaten

1 cup sour cream

1 teaspoon vanilla

3 cups tart apples, peeled
and coarsely chopped

1 prepared 9-inch pie pan
with favorite pastry crust
recipe or a pie crust mix-

CRUMBLE TOPPING

½ cup flour

½ cup brown sugar

1 teaspoon cinnamon

½ teaspoon nutmeg

3 tablespoon chilled butter

Preheat oven to 450° F.

Combine sugar, flour, salt, egg, sour cream, and vanilla and mix. Add the chopped apples and combine. Turn into prepared shell, bake 10 minutes and remove. Reduce oven temperature to 350° F.

Meanwhile, for topping, combine flour, sugar, cinnamon, and nutmeg. Cut in butter with a pastry blender and sprinkle crumb topping over pie. Return to oven and bake for 30 minutes.

SERVES 8

Alice Percival

Breaking into a Fruit Box, 1994, Victor Spinski, American; handbuilt and cast ceramic with glaze, 14 x 11½ x 7½ in. (35.6 x 29.2 x 19.1 cm). Founders Society Purchase with funds from the Modern Decorative Arts Group and Dr. and Mrs. Roger S. Robinson (1994.81).

Fresh Ginger Gingerbread with Chunky Applesauce

1½ cups unbleached white
flour
1 teaspoon baking soda
½ teaspoon salt
1 egg
¼ cup unsulphured molasses
¼ cup dark corn syrup
¼ pound butter, softened
½ cup light brown sugar
½ cup buttermilk at room
temperature
½ cup fresh ginger, grated

APPLESAUCE

2 tablespoons butter
5 medium apples, peeled and
cut into bite-size chunks
1 teaspoon grated lemon zest
1 tablespoon lemon juice
⅛ teaspoon grated nutmeg
½ cup sugar

Preheat oven to 350° F.

Grease an 8-inch square pan. Sift flour, baking soda, and salt together and set aside. Beat the egg in a mixing bowl; add the molasses and corn syrup and mix together. In another bowl, cream the butter and sugar until light and fluffy. Slowly blend with the molasses mixture, mixing well. Alternately add the dry ingredients and buttermilk, beginning and ending with the dry ingredients. Stir in the ginger. Pour batter into prepared pan and bake for 35–40 minutes. Serve warm with applesauce.

For the applesauce, heat butter in large skillet over medium heat. Add apples and lemon zest. Cook, uncovered, until apples are tender, about 10 minutes. Add remaining ingredients and cook for another 5 minutes.

SERVES 6–8

Linda Wells

Ginger-Plum Cobbler

2½ pounds red or purple plums, pitted and halved

3 tablespoons granulated sugar

GINGER TOPPING

1 cup flour

¼ teaspoon baking soda

1 tablespoon ground ginger

7 tablespoons unsalted butter, softened, cut into pieces

3 cups light brown sugar mixed with ⅓ cup granulated sugar

1 tablespoon crystallized ginger, chopped

Preheat the oven to 375° F.

Place the plums, cut-side up, in a baking or gratin dish and sprinkle with granulated sugar.

Combine the flour, baking soda, and ginger in a large bowl. With a pastry blender, a food processor, or an electric mixer, work the butter into the flour mixture until mealy. Add the mixed sugars and crystallized ginger; combine well. Pat the topping evenly over the plums and bake for 30 minutes. Serve warm with a dollop of sour cream.

This dish can be prepared up to 4 hours in advance of serving. Leave in a cool place and reheat in a 350° F oven for 10 minutes.

SERVES 6

Martha Beechler

Lemon Buttermilk Ice

2 cups superfine sugar

½ cup fresh lemon juice

1½ teaspoons grated lemon zest

pinch of salt

1 quart buttermilk

In a large bowl, combine sugar, lemon juice, lemon zest, and salt. Stir to blend. Add buttermilk and stir until sugar dissolves. Cover and refrigerate for 4 hours or overnight. Stir the chilled mixture well. Pour into ice-cream maker and freeze according to manufacturer's instructions.

MAKES 1½ QUARTS

Margie Gillis

Apple Orchard, 1892, George Inness, American; oil on canvas, 30 x 45⅛ in.
(76.2 x 114.6 cm). Gift of Baroness von Ketteler, Henry Ledyard and Hugh
Ledyard, in memory of Henry Brockholst Ledyard (23.100).

Pumpkin Roulade with Maple Filling

6 eggs

2 cups granulated sugar

1⅓ cups canned pumpkin

2 teaspoons lemon juice

1½ cups flour

2 teaspoons baking powder

½ teaspoon salt

4 teaspoons cinnamon

2 teaspoons ground ginger

1 teaspoon nutmeg

1½ cups ground walnuts

MAPLE FILLING

12 ounces cream cheese

½ cup butter

1 tablespoon maple syrup

2 cups confectioners' sugar

Preheat oven to 300° F.

In food processor or mixer, process eggs until thick and lemon-colored. Slowly add sugar, processing until slightly thickened. Add pumpkin and lemon juice. Process until just mixed.

Sift together flour, baking powder, salt, and spices; add to processor. Process until flour is completely incorporated, but do not over-mix. Spread in greased 11 x 16-inch jellyroll pan. Sprinkle top with nuts. Bake approximately 15 minutes or until top springs back to touch.

Turn out onto a towel sprinkled with a little confectioners' sugar, nut side down, and sprinkle sugar on reverse side as well. Roll up cake and towel, lengthwise, with nuts on outside. Cool, seam side down, on a rack. Make filling by blending ingredients until smooth. Unroll cake and spread filling evenly, leaving a ¾-inch unfrosted band along outer edge of the cake's length. Re-roll and chill before serving. Cut slices with very sharp bread knife.

Mary Jane Bostick

Raspberry Crème Anglaise

2 10-ounce packages frozen
   raspberries, thawed
3 eggs, separated
½ cup sugar
grated rind and juice of ½
   lemon
½ cup flour, sifted

Preheat oven to 375° F.

Put the raspberries in the bottom of a 1½-quart casserole.

In a separate bowl, beat the yolks, sugar, lemon rind, and juice together until mixture is very light. Set aside. Beat whites until stiff and place over the yolk mixture. Sift flour over whites and fold all together to thoroughly mix in flour. Spoon mixture over fruit. Bake for 45 minutes. Serve warm with frozen vanilla yogurt or whipped cream.

SERVES 6

Sibley Classen

Strawberries Romanov à la Roostertail

1½ pounds strawberries, cut in
   two (reserve 6 for garnish,
   with stems remaining)
zest and juice of 1 small
   orange, finely grated
2 tablespoons orange-flavored
   liqueur
3 tablespoons sugar
1¼ cups heavy cream

Put the prepared strawberries in a bowl and sprinkle with orange zest and juice, liqueur, and 1 tablespoon sugar. Mix and cover; refrigerate for 1 hour, turning fruit occasionally. Whip the heavy cream until thick. Add remaining sugar and continue whipping until the cream forms soft peaks. Cover and refrigerate until needed. To serve, spoon berries with juice into a glass serving bowl. Pile the whipped cream on top; arrange the garnish berries around the side of the bowl. Let stand for 5 minutes to blend flavors before serving.

SERVES 6

Tom and Diane Schoenith

Frozen Strawberry Meringue Torte

1½ cups graham cracker
crumbs

2 tablespoons butter, melted

½ cup nuts, chopped

2 egg whites at room temperature

½–¾ cup sugar

2 cups fresh or frozen strawberries, crushed

1 tablespoon lemon juice

1 teaspoon vanilla or liqueur
of choice

STRAWBERRY SAUCE

1 10-ounce package frozen
strawberries or 1 cup fresh

3 tablespoons frozen orange
juice or 2 tablespoons
orange marmalade

Preheat oven to 350° F.

Combine crumbs, butter, and nuts. Pat into bottom of a 10-inch springform pan and bake 7–10 minutes. Remove from oven and cool completely. In large bowl, combine egg whites, sugar, berries, lemon juice, and vanilla or liquor; blend on low speed. Increase speed to high and beat until firm peaks form, about 5–10 minutes. Pour into cooled crumb shell and freeze a minimum of 6 hours. Remove from freezer and refrigerate ½ hour before serving. Serve with strawberry sauce.

For the suace, purée the ingredients and serve over or on the side of the torte.

SERVES 12

Malca Wechsler

Centerpiece Strawberry Server and Spoon, ca. 1875, Whiting Manufacturing Company, New York; silver, gilt, height 14 in. (55.6 cm). Founders Society Purchase, Eleanor and Edsel Ford Exhibition and Acquisition Fund (1987.36).

Tiramisu

¼ cup water

¼ cup sugar

6 tablespoons coffee or
   espresso, strong brewed

6 tablespoons brandy

6 tablespoons orange liqueur

1 tablespoon Kahlua

3 egg yolks

2 tablespoons confectioners'
   sugar

8 ounces mascarpone cheese

4 ounces heavy cream,
   whipped

1 package lady fingers

cocoa powder and a square of
   chocolate

Combine water and sugar; heat until sugar is melted. Add coffee and liqueurs and set aside. Beat egg yolks with confectioners' sugar until thick. Beat in cheese and fold in whipped cream. In a 9 x 13-inch dish, line the bottom with ladyfingers that have been dipped in the coffee mixture. Pour the cheese mixture over the ladyfingers. Sift a light sprinkling of cocoa powder over the top and garnish with shaved chocolate (using a vegetable peeler). Refrigerate until ready to serve.

SERVES 8

Mary Roby

Butter Cookies

½ pound butter

½ cup sugar

1⅓ cups flour

1 teaspoon vanilla

raisins or nut pieces (optional)

Preheat oven to 325° F.

Cream together butter and sugar. Add flour and vanilla; mix well. Drop by teaspoonful onto a greased cookie sheet. Each cookie may be trimmed with a raisin or piece of nut. Bake 15 minutes, remove and cool on rack.

MAKES 40–46 SMALL COOKIES

Linda Roeckelein

Orange Slices in White Wine-Ginger Sauce

10 large navel oranges
1 cup ginger marmalade
1 cup stem ginger in syrup
½ cup superfine sugar
1½ cups white wine
½ cup slivered almonds,
   toasted

Peel oranges with a sharp knife, removing all of the white pith. Slice oranges in ¼-inch rounds and place in a glass bowl. In a blender or food processor, with the steel blade in place, combine marmalade, stem ginger, sugar, and wine. Process until completely smooth. Add more sugar as desired. Pour over oranges, cover bowl with plastic wrap, and refrigerate overnight. Turn the oranges occasionally. Before serving, sprinkle toasted almonds over orange slices.

SERVES 8

Jean Hudson

Oranges on a Branch March 14, 1992, 1992, Donald Sultan, American; tar, spackle, and oil on tiles over masonite, 96 x 96 in. (245.8 x 245.8 cm). Founders Society Purchase, Catherine Kresge Dewey Fund, and W. Hawkins Ferry Fund (1994.19).

Cherry Oatmeal Cookies

¾ cup all-purpose flour

½ teaspoon salt

½ teaspoon baking soda

½ cup old-fashioned rolled
oats

1½ sticks (6 ounces) unsalted
butter, softened

⅔ cup granulated sugar

⅔ cup light brown sugar

1 large egg, lightly beaten

1 teaspoon pure vanilla
extract

2 cups pecan pieces
(about 8 ounces)

⅔ cup dried cherries
(about 4 ounces)

Preheat the oven to 350° F.

In a small bowl, whisk together the flour, salt, and baking soda; stir in the oats. In a medium bowl, using an electric mixer, cream the butter with the granulated and brown sugars until light and fluffy. Add the egg and beat thoroughly. Scrape down the bowl with a rubber spatula and beat for another 30 seconds. Mix in the vanilla. Using a rubber spatula, fold in the flour mixture until completely incorporated. Mix in the pecans and cherries.

Line 2 cookie sheets with parchment paper. Form the mixture into balls about 1¼ inches in diameter. Place the balls about 3 inches apart on the prepared cookie sheets.

Bake the cookies 10–12 minutes, or until golden brown and lacy. Let cool completely on the cookie sheets. Using a metal spatula, preferably an icing spatula, transfer the cookies to a plate. The cookies will keep for up to 1 week in an airtight container and for up to 1 month in the freezer.

MAKES 4 DOZEN COOKIES

Margie Gillis

Chocolate Walnut Squares

1 cup butter

½ cup sugar

½ cup brown sugar

1 teaspoon vanilla

2 egg yolks

1 cup flour

1 cup rolled oats

TOPPING

10 plain Hershey's chocolate
bars–or more to taste

2 tablespoons butter

3 cups walnuts, chopped

Preheat oven to 325° F.

Cream butter and sugars. Add vanilla and egg yolks and beat until light. Add flour and rolled oats. Spread on greased cookie sheet, making a large rectangle. Bake 20 minutes or until light brown. Melt chocolate and butter in a double boiler. Spread over crust. Sprinkle with chopped walnuts. Cut while warm. Cool before serving.

SERVES 24

Lynn Miller

Tea Storage Jar, late 16th/early 17th century, Japanese; height: 16⅞ in. (42.8 cm). Founders Society Purchase, New Endowment Fund and Henry Ford II Fund (1989.73).

Cream Wafers

1 cup butter, softened

⅓ cup heavy cream

2 cups flour, sifted

FILLING

¼ cup butter, softened

¾ cup sifted confectioners'
  sugar

1 egg yolk

1 teaspoon vanilla

Mix together butter, cream, and flour. Chill.

Preheat oven to 375° F.

On floured, cloth-covered board, roll out one-third of dough to ⅛-inch thickness, keeping remainder refrigerated until ready to use. Cut into 3-inch rounds. Transfer rounds to sheet of wax paper heavily coated with granulated sugar. Coat each side of rounds with sugar. Place rounds on ungreased baking sheets. Prick with fork about 4 times and bake 7–9 minutes. While cooling, make filling by blending together butter, confectioners' sugar, egg yolk, and vanilla. Spread one cookie round with filling and top with another cookie.

Gayle Shaw Camden

Lemon-Cornmeal Cookies

½ pound (2 sticks) unsalted
    butter
1 scant cup sugar
2 large egg yolks
1½ teaspoons fresh lemon peel,
    finely grated (more if
    desired)
1½ cups all purpose flour
1 cup yellow cornmeal

In a large bowl, cream the butter and sugar. Add the egg yolks, lemon peel, flour, and cornmeal and combine. Shape into a log, 3 inches in diameter for medium cookies and 1½ inches in diameter for small cookies. Wrap in foil and chill in the freezer for at least 10 minutes. (This step can be completed ahead and product stored in refrigerator for several days.) Cut the chilled dough into thin slices. Place them carefully 1 inch apart on buttered baking sheets and bake for 8–10 minutes or until pale golden. Remove from cookie sheets and place on cooling racks.

Cookies can be made up to 3 days ahead and stored in an airtight tin or in the freezer for up to 4 months.

MAKES 40–60 SMALL OR 24 MEDIUM COOKIES

Martha Beechler

Figs 'n Ginger

dried whole figs
roasted, unsalted, shelled pis-
    tachios
candied (crystallized) ginger
    strips

Stuff figs with approximately 2 to 3 pistachios each. Insert ginger strips vertically into figs.

Carl Bunin

Mandelbrot

4 large eggs, room temperature

¾ cup sugar

1 teaspoon almond extract

¾ cup vegetable oil (canola)

3 cups flour

1½ teaspoons baking powder

1 teaspoon cinnamon

½ cup glacé cherries

1½ cups almonds, slivered and
toasted

Preheat oven to 350° F.

Beat eggs well; gradually add sugar while continuing to stir. Add almond extract and oil; beat well. In a separate bowl, combine the flour, baking powder, and cinnamon. Add flour mixture to egg mixture, blending well. Dough will be very stiff. Mix in cherries and slivered almonds.

Grease hands with oil to facilitate handling; divide the dough into 4 long strips each, approximately 3 inches wide, 1 inch thick, and 10 inches long. Bake on cookie sheet lined with parchment paper for 30 minutes. Remove and cut diagonally into ½-inch slices while still warm.

Reduce oven temperature to 175° F. Lay pieces flat on cookie sheet. Sprinkle slices with cinnamon and sugar mixture before toasting. Return to oven for 10–15 minutes, until slightly golden.

Joyce Siegel

Conical Bowl with Leopard Design, 3500/3000 B.C., Iranian; painted earthenware, 3½ x 5 7/16 in. (8.9 x 14 cm). Founders Society Purchase, Henry Ford II Fund, the Catherine Ogdin Estate Fund, Hill Memorial Fund, and the Cleo and Lester Gruber Fund (1995.1).

Nanaimo Bars

¾ cup plus 1 tablespoon butter

¼ cup sugar

⅓ cup cocoa

1 teaspoon vanilla

1 egg

2 cups graham wafer crumbs

1 cup coconut, finely chopped

2 tablespoons vanilla instant
pudding powder

3 tablespoons milk

2 cups sifted confectioners'
sugar

3 ounces semisweet chocolate

Melt ½ cup butter in saucepan. Blend in sugar, cocoa, vanilla, egg, graham wafer crumbs, and coconut. Press into 9-inch square pan. Chill.

Cream remaining one-quarter cup butter. Blend in pudding powder, milk, and confectioners' sugar. Spread over graham wafer crust and chill again. Melt chocolate and 1 tablespoon butter. Spread over chilled mixture and refrigerate.

Keep chilled and cut into squares as needed.

MAKES 16–20 BARS

Lucie Kelly

White Chocolate Brownies

12 ounces butter

14 ounces white chocolate,
chopped

7 eggs

¼ teaspoon salt

1¾ cups sugar

2 tablespoons vanilla

3½ cups flour

1 cup chocolate chips

Preheat oven to 350° F.

Melt together butter and white chocolate. Let cool. Beat eggs with 4 teaspoon salt until blended. Add the sugar slowly to the eggs, beating 5–7 minutes until fluffy. Add the cooled chocolate mixture to the eggs and beat thoroughly. Add vanilla and blend. Mix in the flour thoroughly. Fold in chocolate chips and spread the batter evenly in a greased 12 x 17-inch pan. Bake in oven until lightly browned, 20–25 minutes. Cool and cut into 1½-inch squares.

MAKES 54–60

Algie Flaviani

Index

Michigan Fruits and Vegetables, east wall, *Detroit Industry*, 1932, Diego Rivera, Mexican; fresco, 26¼ x 72⅞ in. (68 x 185 cm). Gift of Edsel B. Ford (33.10).

Michigan Fruits and Veg-etables, **east wall,** *Detroit Industry*, **1952, Diego Rivera, Mexican; fresco, 26¼ x 72⅞ in. (68 x 185 cm). Gift of Edsel B. Ford (33.10).**

COLOPHON

This book is composed mostly in
Adobe Walbaum on a Macintosh G3 Powerbook in QuarkXpress.

This classic metal typeface was cut in the late 1930s, for
Monotype Corporation, for both machine composition and display use.
Typefaces similar to Walbaum, inspired by the work of French
typographer Firmin Didot, began to appear in Germany after 1800.
The original source for this font is attributed to Didot, based on
alphabets he designed in the late 18th century.